THE Papercraft
WEEKEND WORKBOOK

THE Papercraft
WEEKEND WORKBOOK

From Ribbons to Rose Petals, Creative Techniques
for Making 50 Stunning Projects

FIONA JONES

Reader's Digest

The Reader's Digest Association, Inc.
Pleasantville, New York/Montreal/London/Hong Kong

To my family and friends for all the love and support they have given me throughout the years.

A READER'S DIGEST BOOK
This edition published by The Reader's Digest Association
by arrangement with Cico Books

FOR CICO BOOKS
Photography: Tino Tedaldi
Editor: Katie Hardwicke
Design: Sara Kidd

FOR READER'S DIGEST
U.S. Project Editor: Marilyn J. Knowlton
Canadian Project Editor: Pamela Johnson
Associate Art Director: George McKeon
Cover design: Amanda Wilson
Executive Editor, Trade Publishing: Dolores York
Vice President & Publisher, Trade Publishing: Harold Clarke

Library of Congress Cataloging-in-Publication Data

Jones, Fiona.
   Papercraft weekend workbook : from ribbons to rose petals – creative
techniques for making over 50 stunning projects / Fiona Jones.
        p. cm.
   Includes index.
   ISBN 0-7621-0627-1
   1. Paper work. 2. House furnishings —Design and construction — Amateurs'
manuals. I. Title.
TT870.J664 2006
745.54—dc22
                                                    2005044531

Printed in China

Address any comments about
The Papercraft Weekend Workbook to:
The Reader's Digest Association, Inc.
Adult Trade Publishing
Reader's Digest Road
Pleasantville, NY 10570-7000

For more Reader's Digest products and information, visit our website:
www.rd.com (in the United States)
www.rd.ca (in Canada)
www.rdasia.com.hk (in Hong Kong)

10 9 8 7 6 5 4 3 2 1

Contents

Introduction

I have been crafting for as long as I can remember. Most of my hobbies in childhood were craft-orientated, and with the hectic lifestyles we all lead these days, I find that crafting can be very therapeutic. Whether enjoying the social benefits of crafting with friends or the meditational qualities of crafting alone, I firmly believe that there is at least one craft for everyone to enjoy—the only problem is finding the one for you. Papercrafts covers a wide spectrum of techniques, and with the huge range of papers available to the crafter these days, it can be a very enjoyable pastime.

The projects in this book are all paper-based and can be individually completed within a weekend. Each project has a list of the materials needed and an indicator as to the level of difficulty, the technique(s) used, and length of time needed to complete it. There are three grades of difficulty: beginner—suitable for anyone, even those new to crafting; intermediate—for those who have some experience with crafting; and advanced—these projects require a reasonable amount of crafting knowledge and dexterity. However, anyone, whatever his or her experience or ability, can complete any of the projects by following the step-by-step instructions.

Those new to crafting may wish to start with a simpler project before progressing to a more advanced one. For example, the "Tissue Box" project (see pages 16–19) guides you through the process of papermaking, while the "Wedding Stationery" project (see pages 114–117) assumes you know the basics of papermaking and takes the process a step further.

The times given for each project are an approximate guide, since everyone works at his or her own pace. It is wise not to rush—take your time and enjoy the process of creating. The hours do include drying times except for projects that include papermaking. When making paper, you will achieve a better result if you allow it to dry slowly. It is generally best to leave the paper overnight—set aside one day for making your paper and complete the project the following day.

Within this book you will find many techniques, some that you may recall enjoying as a child, such as collage, papier-mâché, and paper cutting; and others that may be new to you, such as kirigami, paper quilling, napkin decoupage, and altered art. Even classic papercraft techniques, such as origami, have something to offer the modern-day crafter, and they are often the inspiration for many other popular crafts, such as tea-bag folding, iris folding, and kirigami.

All the techniques in this book can be used on other projects—the only limitation is your imagination. There is no reason why you can't have a marbled lamp shade, a scrapbook coaster, quilled Christmas decorations, or even a quilted picture frame. After countless workshops the biggest problem I have encountered is people's fear of making a mistake. In crafting there are no mistakes, only happy accidents. When things don't go as planned, you generally discover something new from the process. Once you get past your fear, you will find that the world is your oyster and anything is possible. Have the confidence to experiment and, most of all, have fun!

Tools

Every crafter needs a basic tool kit, one that he or she always has at hand when crafting. This should include such essential tools as a craft knife, metal-edge rule, cutting mat, and scissors, together with a selection of brushes, pencils, and adhesive.

Equipment

Craft knife This is indispensable for cutting straight lines, templates, and trimming and shaping. Keep spare blades, especially when papercrafting, as it is important to have a sharp blade in order to achieve a smooth, clean cut—a blunt blade could snag or tear your paper.

Scissors There is a wide variety of scissors available, each designed for various purposes. Small ones with a fine point are ideal for getting into tight corners when cutting detailed decoupage prints, while spring-loaded snips are easier on the hands for general cutting. Decorative-edged scissors are great for embellishing paper.

Sharp pencil Another vital piece of equipment for marking up projects and measuring. A mechanical pencil with separate leads is ideal, as it is always sharp and gives a fine line.

CRAFTER'S TIP

If you craft with a group of friends, you could always purchase an expensive piece of equipment, such as a die-cut machine, between you, or alternatively make sure that you all buy different dies and share them.

Crafting tools, such as punches or a ribbler, are invaluable.

Embossing tool This is a versatile tool that is good for stencil embossing and also for scoring paper or card before folding it. Embossing tools come in different sizes with a small and a large end—invest in a couple to give yourself a good range. When scoring a card before folding, always score the outside of the fold because this will give you a better finish.

Tweezers Many crafters find a pair of tweezers invaluable when trying to position peel-off stickers and gems or other small items.

Single-needle tool Useful when paper pricking—an ordinary needle can tire your fingers.

Light box A useful tool not just for embossing but also for transferring designs and tracing text, templates, or patterns. There are some inexpensive, small-scale light boxes available from craft suppliers that are ideal for card making and other small projects.

Additional items Two other "tools" worth having in your basic kit are paintbrushes and alcohol-free baby wipes. Brushes can be a great way to sprinkle glitter or powder over specific areas of your work and can be used for brushing away unwanted powder. Baby wipes are fabulous for cleaning all sorts of things, including your stamps. You may also find papercrafting uses for some tools borrowed from other areas of your home, such as plastic wrap and a blender from your kitchen, small wood saws and drills used for modeling projects, or a sewing machine.

Adhesives

Almost every crafting project requires an adhesive of some sort. In your craft store you will find that there are adhesives for just about everything—from double-sided tape, low-tack tape, and masking tape to PVA glue, industrial-strength glue, and spray adhesive. There are adhesives especially designed to stick specific surfaces, such as decoupage glue, metal glue, vellum tape, and acid-free glue. Vellums are notoriously difficult to stick, since PVA glue is too wet and buckles the vellum, and double-sided tape shows through. So manufacturers have developed special vellum tapes, which apply a dry glue that does not show through. When using paper or lightweight card, it is wise to avoid PVA, as it will warp the paper. Instead, use either double-sided tape or a dry-glue applicator machine.

Crafting tools

There are so many other useful crafting tools, such as punches and decorative-edged scissors, to choose from that you'll have a wide choice. Invest in one or two that you think you will use the most and then slowly build up your collection, buying additional equipment as and when required.

Ribbler This small machine allows you to create a corrugated effect on any paper or card strong enough to hold its shape.

Dry-adhesive and die-cut machines give you many options.

Die-cut machines Available in various makes and sizes—investigate the range of dies that are available for each before making a purchase.

Stencils These are the best way to achieve an embossed effect on card. If using light-colored card, you can use brass or acetate stencils on a light source, such as a light box or against a window on a sunny day. Lay the stencil down and position your card facedown over the top. Use a clear candle to rub over the back of the card to allow the embossing tool to glide over the surface and then gently push the card into the recesses. If using dark-colored card, you will find it easier if you invest in a stenciling system that gives you two stencils—one below your card and one above to show you where to emboss.

Eyeletting tools These vary depending on the manufacturer. Some involve a hammer with separate hole-making and eyelet-setting tools, while others have spring-loaded mechanisms. The spring-loaded tools are more expensive, but some crafters find them easier and safer to use than the separate hammer design. They all come with different-sized ends to allow you to set a range of small-to-large eyelets.

Materials

The type of materials and some specialized tools that you require will be dependent upon the project and the techniques used. However, you will soon find that your basic supplies will expand after every trip to the craft store until you have a good supply on hand.

Stamps and inks

Most crafters have at least one or two rubber stamps, and often many more, because they are so versatile. They can be combined with a huge range of ink pads and embossing powders to create special effects. You can even use some for paper casting. The ink pads come in three main types: dye based, pigment ink, and permanent.

Dye ink pads Made of water-based ink that dries quickly. The stamped image will run if it gets wet.

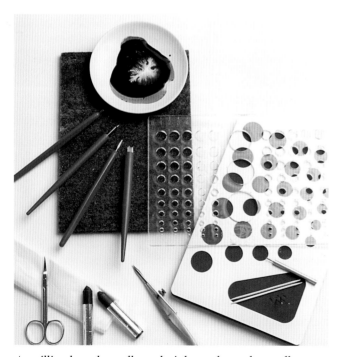

A quilling board, needle tools, inks, and pastels are all specialized tools required for certain techniques.

Pigment ink pads Glycerine-based and do not evaporate and so take longer to dry. This allows you time to pour on some embossing powder, tip off the excess, and melt it with the useful and versatile embossing heat tool. Never use the embossing heat tool on your cutting mat, as it will warp.

Permanent ink pads Consist of permanent ink. Some will stamp onto any surface, even acetate and metal, and most are quick-drying.

Specialized tools

Some crafts, such as parchment craft and quilling, require specialized tools. There is a complete range of products for parchment from different-shaped needle tools to felt pads, snips, and inks.

You will find making uniform quilled coils easier if you use a quilling tool and board, but it can be done with a toothpick and waxed paper.

For stenciling, a stencil cutter is a fine hot-point tool similar to one used in pyrography (wood-burning). It is the easiest way to produce stencils from acetate, but you can also use a craft knife.

Artist's materials

Color pencils are invaluable for coloring in stamped images, and you can use any oil pastels to color vellum, blending the colors with a tissue and a drop of parchment blending oil or white spirit. You can use paints in a similar way to color in images or add an overall background color.

Other mediums include varnish to seal projects; acrylic paints, some of which are acid-free; inks; and decorating chalks that are the same as artist's chalks, only in palette form for ease of use.

Embellishments

Often projects do not look finished until they have that little extra embellishment, and this is where you can really add a touch of individuality.

Brads and eyelets These come in a vast range of sizes, colors, and shapes and are great for fixing difficult materials such as vellums. Other metal items, such as charms, clips, and locks, are widely available in scrapbooking ranges.

Glitters, sequins, and beads Pots of glitter, both chunky and ultrafine, confetti, sequins, beads, and gems can be sprinkled over, stuck on, inserted, and embedded in paints and glues.

Other craft items These include peel-offs, stickers, and rub-ons (transfers), but you can use other small items to accessorize an article too, such as old coins and postage stamps.

Fibers There is a wide range of fibers and mesh available from fluffy wools and fur trims to luxurious threads, delicate lace, and beautiful fabric and paper ribbons.

Dried or pressed flowers These can add that natural touch and are readily available from craft stores in an incredible range of flower varieties. Alternatively, you can press your own either in a microwave flower press in double-quick time or in a traditional flower press. White flowers are notoriously difficult to press quickly and will need the old-fashioned treatment. Mini silk or paper

Pencils, paints, and chalks will add a flourish of color.

flowers, made in a wide range of colors, are an alternative 3-D version.

Gilding wax and leaf metals Designed for surfaces such as wood, gilding wax can be applied sparingly to card and paper and left for a few minutes to soak in before buffing up to give a luxurious effect. Leaf metals are applied using a glue size and may need to be lacquered or varnished to stop them from tarnishing.

Webbing spray and 3-D paints These add a raised dimension to your work and are easy to use.

Pearly powders Rub on with a finger or mix with other mediums. Similar to chalks, these need to be fixed with fixative or hair spray to stop them from rubbing off. Pigment powders are water soluble and so can be used like paint.

CRAFTER'S TIP

When looking for embellishments, you'll be amazed at what you can find in antique shops—from old postcards and coins to lace and beaded necklaces just waiting to be dismantled for that next craft project.

Paper

Paper is such a versatile medium. It is normally made from wood pulp, but you will also find paper in which other plants have been used, such as bamboo, walnuts, bagasse, cotton, kozo, and hemp, to name but a few. With such an array of machine- and handmade papers, no crafter should be lost for inspiration, and you can even make it yourself for something truly unique.

Colored paper and card Useful for a wide variety of projects, this should form the basis of your paper collection. It ranges from plain machine-made card stock, which is generally inexpensive, to metallics, holographics, pearlescents, and glitters. Most have a plain finish, but some are embossed, embroidered, or textured. There is an ever-increasing range of printed and decorative papers, and this is partly owing to the rising popularity of scrapbooking. When card making, you can use wrapping papers and even packaging, including candy wrappers.

Mountboard A very thick card that was originally designed for framing pictures. It usually has a white base to which a colored surface has been applied. When papercrafting, you will find it a versatile material that you can use whenever a strong foundation is required.

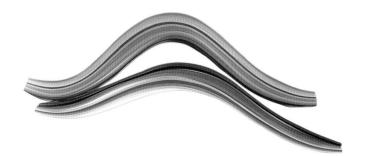

Quilling strips are precut and come in a rainbow of colors.

Watercolor paper A strong paper that comes in a variety of weights and finishes. Cold and hot press refer to how the finish has been achieved—whether it has been passed between cold or hot rollers. Cold-pressed, or "not" ("not hot-pressed"), tends to have a slightly textured surface, while hot-pressed is smoother. This paper is sized with gelatin to allow it to take a lot of moisture without buckling too much.

Tissue paper, crepe paper, and napkins Tissue paper tears easily and takes on translucent qualities when glued or varnished. The stronger crepe has a crinkled look and can be stretched and molded. Napkins, like tissue, are very lightweight and can have fabulous printed designs ideal for many crafting projects. Wet-strength tissue paper has been treated to stop it from disintegrating when wet, allowing you to color it yourself.

Mulberry paper One of the first specialty papers, mulberry paper has become a household favorite with many crafters. It is a fibrous paper that is made from the kozo fibers taken from the outer branches of the mulberry tree.

Silk paper A soft cotton paper with an almost fabriclike feel that is derived from the long silk fibers it contains.

Vellum One of the first papers invented, traditionally made from animal skin and called parchment, today vellum is commercially manufactured by machine. It comes in a range of colors, along with patterns and designs, and is perfect for parchment craft.

Origami and quilling paper There are other papers that have been specially designed for particular crafts, such as origami, tea-bag folding, and quilling. Origami and tea-bag papers are especially lightweight, allowing them to be folded many times to create intricate patterns. Quilling papers come in various colors and have been precision cut into thin strips approximately 12 in. (30 cm) long.

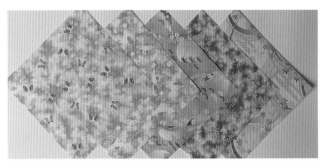

Origami papers are perfect for Oriental-themed projects.

Japanese lace paper Usually white and as light as tissue paper, this paper has patterned holes in it that give it a lacelike quality. Washi is another Japanese paper. It is considered to be one of the thinnest yet toughest papers available.

Handmade papers They tend to be thicker and stiffer than other papers and are made worldwide. Many handmade papers come from countries such as India, Nepal, and Japan, where papermaking is a tradition going back hundreds of years. Indian rag paper is made from cotton fibers and is a thick, strong paper with ragged or deckle edges. Batik paper is a handmade paper that has been decorated using batik techniques of creating a resist pattern with wax before coloring.

Other materials There are some materials that are paperlike, but not strictly paper. For example, there are a variety of meshes, foams, and paper-backed flannel papers that contain plastic to give them strength, flexibility, and texture. Acetate is a transparent plastic and is available in different types. They have varying water contents, and some will curl when they come in contact with moisture. Shrink plastic comes in a limited range of brittle plastic sheets and die cuts that can be decorated before being heated to shrink.

Papermaking

Papermaking is a very satisfying pastime, and just about anyone can do it. You will need a tub or vat partially filled with water in which to suspend your pulp. A frame and mesh are necessary to collect each sheet of paper, and drying sheets or cloths are needed to support the pulp while it dries. There are papermaking kits available that contain two sizes of frame, measuring 5 x 7 in. (13 x 18 cm) and 8½ x 11 in. (21 x 30 cm), together with other essential pieces of equipment, such as meshes and drying sheets.

You can make your own pulp by cutting up and liquidizing bought paper or using cotton linter sheets, which consist of dried cotton pulp in sheet form ready for easy reconstituting. There are also molds available for use with cotton linter squares.

A sieve and jug are vital for rescuing your pulp when you have finished making paper. If you are planning on making more paper in a matter of days, place the pulp in a tub with a little water and refrigerate until needed. If you don't think you'll need it for a while, either freeze it or squeeze out as much water as possible, form it into balls, and then leave them to dry.

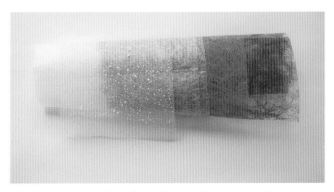

Plain or decorated mesh can be used in papercraft.

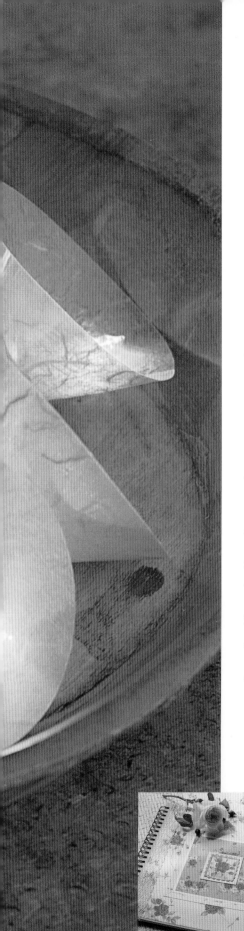

Accessories for the Home

Y ou'll be amazed at how many items around the house can be decorated or even made entirely from paper. From coasters and lamp shades to picture frames and decorative containers, you'll find this chapter full of wonderful ideas to accent your home, whether it be for a special event or everyday use. Explore the pleasures of working with papers, such as tissue, crepe, silk, and even napkins or, better still, have fun making your own. This can be very satisfying and is rather like baking a cake, as the results depend entirely on the ingredients you use. The one thing you can be sure of is that each sheet of paper will be absolutely unique.

Tissue box

A decorative holder covered in handmade paper is a great way to disguise a functional tissue box. The basic instructions for handmade paper provided here can be used in other projects in this book. The better-quality paper you use, the better finish your handmade paper will have, so don't be tempted to use newspapers, magazines, or junk mail.

TECHNIQUES: Papermaking and collage **LEVEL:** Beginner **TIME:** 6–7 hours (plus drying time for paper)

MATERIALS NEEDED
For handmade paper:
- Bowl, sieve, and wooden spoon
- Assorted colored and white papers
- Jug
- Blender
- Paper shredder (optional)
- Vat of water
- PVA glue and teaspoon
- Inclusions (see Step 4)
- Papermaking frame and drying sheets
- Towels and an old board or tray

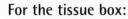

For the tissue box:
- Papier-mâché tissue box
- Matte cream spray paint
- Handmade paper using white, yellow, and orange pulp with marigold petals, corn-silk filaments, daisies, and skeleton leaves
- PVA glue
- Brush and water
- Craft knife
- Cream, yellow, and brown paper cords
- Matte varnish spray

1 **TO MAKE THE PAPER:** Prepare the paper pulp by ripping approximately 10 sheets of paper into 1-in. (2.5-cm) squares, or use a paper shredder. Place them in a bowl, cover with water, and leave overnight. (You can speed up this process by soaking the pieces for 1 hour in warm water, but this will weaken your finished paper slightly.)

2 Pour 17 fl. oz. (500 ml) warm water into a blender and add a ball of paper the size of a golf ball. Process the mixture until there are no visible bits of paper left; then drain the pulp through a sieve. Place the pulp in a bowl, adding a little water to stop it from drying out. Repeat for the rest of the paper.

3 Half-fill a vat with water and add a teaspoon of PVA glue to strengthen the finished paper and help hold the inclusions. Add 2 to 3 handfuls of pulp, depending on how thick you want the paper to be—you can always add more pulp if the first sheet is too thin.

4 Small decorations (such as petals, dried herbs, confetti, or glitter), perfume oils, and fabric dyes can be added at this stage. For larger decorations, such as whole pressed flowers and skeleton leaves, drop them onto each sheet (at the end of Step 6) before all the water has drained off.

5 Stir the mixture thoroughly; then place the frame vertically in the water at the back of the vat.

6 Slide the frame downward so that it lies flat on the bottom of the vat before carefully lifting it up, keeping it horizontal. To create an average sheet of paper, the pulp should be approximately ⅛ in. (3 mm) thick. Add another handful of pulp after every second sheet and stir well to maintain the same thickness.

7 Allow the water to drain away, giving the frame a gentle shake from side to side. Tilt it slightly to allow any excess water to drain off. Open the frame and carefully remove the mesh.

8 Place the mesh pulp side up on a folded towel. Cover first with a plastic drying sheet, then with an old board or tray. Stand on it for 10 seconds; then remove the tray and peel away the mesh. Dry at room temperature for 6 to 10 hours; then bend the drying sheet back to pop off the paper.

9 **TO COVER THE TISSUE BOX:** Prepare the papier-mâché tissue box by spraying it with matte cream spray paint. Make your own paper, as in Steps 1 to 8, using white, yellow, and a little orange pulp, with marigold petals and corn-silk filaments mixed in, along with embedded daisies and skeleton leaves.

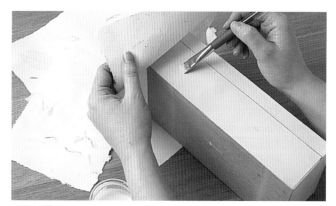

10 Smear PVA glue over one end of the box, with the lid in place, and stick the first sheet of handmade paper in position. Apply more glue before wrapping the sheet around the sides of the box. Carefully cut along the edge of the lid with a sharp craft knife to separate the lid and the base.

11 To stop the corners from becoming too bulky with several layers of paper, remove the excess from the sheet by wetting a tear line with a brush and water and gently pulling.

12 Continue to cover the box in the same way with randomly placed paper. Re-create the tissue opening by wetting around the edges of the aperture and gently pulling the excess paper away.

13 Add a trim of three color-coordinated twisted paper cords, stuck in place with PVA glue. If you want to protect your box from wear and tear, it is a good idea to spray it with matte varnish.

CRAFTER'S TIP

You can prepare paper pulp in advance. To store it before use, either place it in a watertight container and freeze it or squeeze out all the excess water and form into small balls, then dry. Allow to defrost or soak overnight, depending on your preferred method, before use.

Beaded coasters

Delight your dinner guests with these beautiful, easy-to-make beaded coasters —perfect for a celebratory glass of champagne. For special occasions you could color-coordinate them by using different papers and beads to complement your table linen. You could even create a set of matching place mats.

TECHNIQUE: Collage **LEVEL:** Intermediate **TIME:** 3–4 hours

MATERIALS NEEDED:
- MDF coaster base
- Drill (if the coasters are not predrilled)
- Countersink
- Ruler
- Gold and silver metallic tissue papers
- PVA glue
- Brushes
- Silver leaf
- Gold mica flakes
- Clear gloss varnish
- Beading needle
- Flower beads
- Multicolored metallic beads
- Color-coordinating thread
- Sticky tape
- Self-adhesive clear plastic bumpers
- Gold glitter card
- Cutting mat, craft knife, and scissors

1 Drill and countersink holes in the corners of the coaster. Measure and drill three more holes, evenly spaced on each side. Make sure you protect your work surface while doing this.

2 Take a piece of silver metallic tissue paper larger than your coaster and, using PVA glue, stick it over the top of the coaster.

3 Gently ease the metallic tissue paper into the drilled holes, using the tail end of the paintbrush.

4 Apply PVA glue to the coaster edges and stick the paper over the sides, folding it at the corners. Trim the paper to ¼ in. (6 mm) and stick it down.

5 Tear shapes of gold and silver tissue, and stick them randomly across the face of the coaster, folding over at the edges. Leave to dry.

6 Lightly brush patches of PVA glue across the top of the coaster; then leave it to one side for 10 to 15 minutes to become tacky.

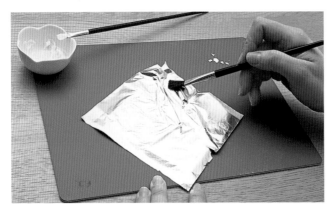

7 Lay a sheet of silver leaf over the top of the coaster and gently press down with a soft brush. Use small, circular movements with your brush to remove any excess silver.

8 Take some gold mica flakes and stick them randomly across the surface with PVA glue.

9 Coat the top of the coaster with clear gloss varnish to seal, making sure not to leave a pool of varnish in the holes. When dry, apply another coat of varnish and leave to dry before proceeding with the next step.

10 Thread the needle and stick the end of the thread to the back of the coaster with a piece of sticky tape. Take the thread up through a corner hole, then through a flower bead and a metallic bead. Take it back down through the flower bead and coaster hole before moving on to the next hole. Work around the coaster, keeping the thread as tight as possible.

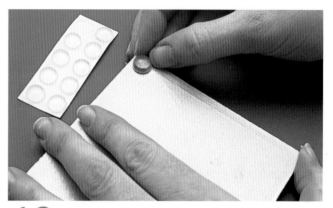

11 Having finished the last hole, fasten the thread with another small piece of tape and trim the excess. Cut a piece of gold glitter card slightly smaller than the coaster.

12 Brush PVA glue over the base of the coaster and stick it to the card. Stick self-adhesive bumpers at each corner.

CRAFTER'S TIP

You can purchase mica, silver leaf, and copper leaf by the sheet from craft stores. However, for a touch of ultimate luxury, use gold leaf, which is surprisingly inexpensive. Applying a thin coat of clear varnish or lacquer prevents the leaf from tarnishing.

Keepsake scrapbook album

There are many patterned and plain papers produced by scrapbook manufacturers, especially designed to complement one another. When scrapbooking, don't forget to decorate your album cover as well. The rose pattern used here with lace trimming lends itself to creating a keepsake album that reflects a bygone era. A truly special place to store precious memories.

1 Take a piece of cotton linter slightly larger than the paper-cast mold and wet it. Lay the cotton linter over the mold and carefully push it into the crevices using the round end of a paintbrush handle.

2 Stick a 12-in. (30-cm) square of large-rose paper to the front of the scrapbook. Cut a 1¾-in. (4.5-cm) square of small-rose paper and cut it in half diagonally. Use acid-free adhesive to trim the long edge of both triangles with lace.

3 Glue the triangles to the two outer corners of the cover, wrapping the lace around the edge and sticking on the reverse. Stick a 15-in. (38-cm) length of lace down the ring-bound edge and glue the ends on the reverse. Stick the first page to the inside front cover.

4 Layer the square of bouquet paper on the square of cream paper. Cut four ½-in. (13-mm) strips of small-rose paper. Fix to the cream paper with double-sided tape, overlapping the corners.

5 Use a craft knife and ruler to miter the corners. Stick extra tape on the back of the cream square. Remove the backing strips from the tape and attach the square in the center of the cover.

6 Lightly pat a dampened tea bag over the paper cast. Let it dry before trimming. Cut a 2-in. (5-cm) square of large-rose paper and glue in the center. Stick the cast on the center of the cover.

TECHNIQUES: Scrapbooking and paper casting **LEVEL:** Beginner **TIME:** 5–6 hours

MATERIALS NEEDED:

- Cotton linter
- Paper-cast mold
- Paintbrush and water
- Cream rose-patterned paper: one sheet with large flowers and two sheets with small flowers
- Scrapbook
- Lace trimming
- Acid-free glue and double-sided tape
- 6-in. (15-cm) square of green rose bouquet paper
- 6½-in. (17-cm) square of plain cream paper
- Tea bag
- Scissors, craft knife, cutting mat, and ruler

Papier-mâché rose bowl

Bring a touch of summer into your home with this delightful potpourri bowl. You can have the scent of roses all year-round, or use your own favorite perfume if you prefer.

TECHNIQUES: Papier-mâché and scented papermaking **LEVEL:** Intermediate **TIME:** 6–7 hours (plus drying time)

MATERIALS NEEDED

For the bowl:
- Pencil
- Pink silk paper
- Paintbrush and water
- Glass or plastic bowl, to use as a mold, approx. 6 x 4 in. (15 x 10 cm)
- Tall drinking glass
- PVA glue and sticky tape
- Green mulberry paper
- Pink mesh paper
- Pink silk roses
- Craft knife, cutting mat, and ruler

For the potpourri:
- Papermaking equipment (see page 16)
- Masking tape
- Pink and lilac paper and tracing paper for pulp
- Rose perfume extract

1 In pencil, draw a large petal shape 1½ times the height of the mold on the pink silk paper. Paint over the pencil line with water; then gently tear out the petal shape. Repeat to make another eight petals; then make three smaller petals (the height of the mold) in the same way.

2 Place the mold on a sheet of silk paper. "Draw" around it with a wet paintbrush and gently tear out the circle. Repeat twice. Stick one of the circles to the outer base of the mold with a loop of sticky tape.

3 Using PVA glue, stick the three small petals to the base circle, overlapping as you go. Pleat them around the bottom to shape them to the mold. (Be careful not to use too much PVA glue, as it will soak through the paper.) It helps to rest the mold on an upturned glass to raise it above the work surface.

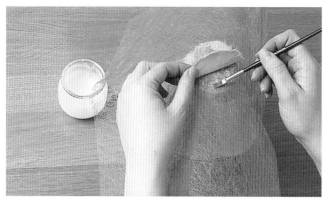

4 Stick a second circle on the base, followed by a 13½-in. (34-cm) square of pink mesh on top. Stick the third circle on top of this to hold the mesh in place and strengthen the base.

5 Create two pleats at each corner of the mesh to shape it to fit around the mold. Temporarily secure these with more sticky tape.

6 Removing the tape as you go, stick overlapping silk paper strips, about 1 in. (2.5 cm) wide, all around the mesh, wetting and tearing the top edges. Cover with a second layer of strips and leave to dry.

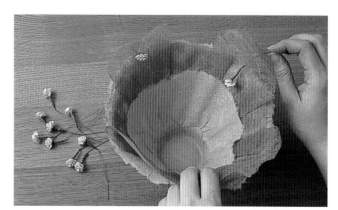

7 Remove the bowl from the mold and fold each corner of the mesh over, threading a silk rose through to secure it.

8 Apply a third layer of strips around the bowl, fixing the rose stems in position with more strips of silk paper.

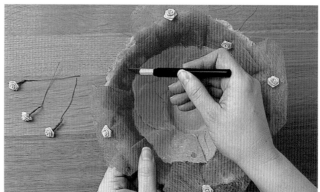

9 Use a craft knife to make tiny holes near the top of the bowl equidistant between the roses. Thread more roses through the holes, fixing with more strips of paper.

10 Take four large petals and space them evenly around the bowl, overlapping as you go. Fix them in position with PVA glue.

11 Once again, pleat the petals at the base to fit the shape of the mold and glue in place.

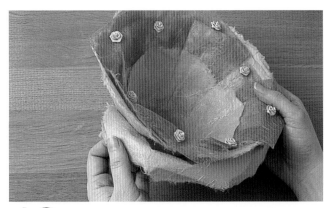

12 Repeat Steps 10 and 11 with another five large petals, curling the edges outward.

13 With a brush and water, tear a star-shaped calyx from green mulberry paper. Stick this around the base of the bowl with PVA glue.

14 Make your own potpourri by creating petal shapes on the papermaking mesh with masking tape. Follow the papermaking instructions on pages 16 to 18, adding rose perfume extract to the vat. When the petals are half dry, remove them from the drying boards and curl them.

CRAFTER'S TIP

You will find it easier and quicker to make the papier-mâché bowl if you allow the PVA glue to thicken before use. Pour a little into a dish, leave it in a warm place to thicken, allowing some water to evaporate from it before covering the dish with plastic food wrap.

Decoupaged tray

Decoupage is a traditional and easy way to decorate household objects to great effect. Use a large photograph of a garden scene as the background to create a tray that is perfect for carrying glasses and a pitcher of home-made lemonade for a lazy summer day in the garden.

TECHNIQUE: Decoupage **LEVEL:** Beginner **TIME:** 4–5 hours

MATERIALS NEEDED:
- Wooden tray
- Handmade grass paper
- Decoupage glue
- Flat brush
- Photo of a garden scene
- White tissue paper
- Pressed flowers
- Gloss varnish
- Craft knife, cutting mat, and ruler

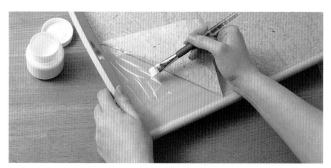

1 Cut a piece of grass paper to fit the base of the tray and stick in position with decoupage glue.

2 Use more decoupage glue to stick your chosen photo in the center of the tray.

3 Cut two 2-in. (5-cm)-wide strips of white tissue the height of the tray. Spread decoupage glue over the grass paper on either side of the photo and stick the tissue strips in position. Leave to dry.

4 Coat the base of the tray with decoupage glue using horizontal strokes. Leave to dry. Apply another coat of glue to the tray base, this time using vertical strokes.

5 While still wet, stick pressed flowers down each tissue strip. Leave to dry. Apply two or three coats of gloss varnish over the entire surface of the tray (back and front) to seal it and to prevent staining. Leave to dry between coats.

Butterfly
lamp shade

Follow these simple instructions to create a decorative lamp shade. Once you have cut out the template, you can easily make as many shades as you like, so you can change them to suit your mood. Alternatively, you could create a theme with them to tie in with party decorations for a special event.

TECHNIQUES: Papercutting and punching **LEVEL:** Beginner **TIME:** 1–2 hours

MATERIALS NEEDED:
- Night-light lamp
- Patterned paper
- Scrap paper
- Compass
- Butterfly paper punch
- Masking tape
- Narrow double-sided tape
- Scissors
- Cutting mat, ruler, pencil, and craft knife

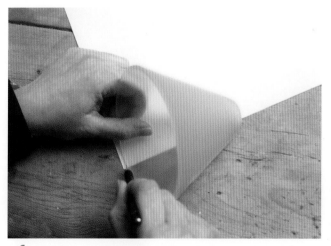

1 Lay the patterned paper facedown on the work surface and place the lamp shade along the edge. Mark the top and bottom of the shade.

2 Lay a ruler on top of the shade and mark the point where it touches the paper. Place the point of the compass on this mark and use the other two marks to draw the two arcs.

3 Using scissors, carefully cut out the shape. Cut another shape out of scrap paper and save to use as a template later.

4 Place the patterned paper facedown on the shade and mark the edge with a pencil. Remove it, and leaving a ½-in. (13-mm) overlap, cut away the excess.

5 Having repeated Step 4 with the template, ignoring the overlap, fold it in half. Then fold it in half twice more.

6 Using a pencil and the template, mark the folds on the reverse of the patterned paper.

CRAFTER'S TIP

For a decorative edge, use a hole punch and eyelet setter to fix eight eyelets around the top edge of the shade. Use your template (as made in Step 3) to place them equidistantly. Thread some color-coordinated ribbon through the eyelets and fix on the inside of the shade with double-sided tape.

CRAFTER'S TIP

Instead of butterflies, punch a few dragonflies from a sheet of iridescent paper and stick their bodies to the lamp shade, leaving their wings and tails free, giving the impression of dragonflies in flight.

7 Place the punch beside the first mark and punch out a butterfly. Punch out three more butterflies using every other mark as a guide.

8 Use masking tape to shorten the length of the punch. Use the remaining four marks to punch out more butterflies.

9 Place double-sided tape down one edge of the paper lamp shade and, using the glass shade as a guide, stick the paper edges together.

10 Take four punched butterflies and stick tiny pieces of double-sided tape to the body of each one, on the patterned side. Position at the top of the shade.

Picture frame with memento window

Many of us like to display photos taken at special events to remind us of happy occasions. This project shows you how to create a frame with a difference, using the technique of paper weaving. It also includes a window, allowing you to display a small memento connected to the event.

TECHNIQUES: Paper weaving and window making **LEVEL:** Advanced **TIME:** 5–6 hours

MATERIALS NEEDED:

- Assorted papers
- Self-adhesive mountboard
- White mountboard
- Small piece of fabric
- Sheet of acetate slightly smaller than the frame
- ½ x ¼-in. (13 x 6-mm) balsa-wood strip
- Masking tape
- PVA glue and paintbrush
- Double-sided tape
- Scissors
- Low-tack tape (optional)
- Embellishments (optional)
- Craft knife, cutting mat, and ruler

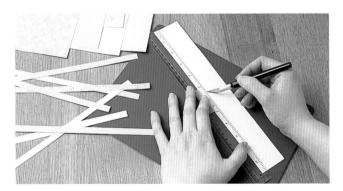

1 Cut ⅜-in. (1-cm) strips of decorative papers approximately 12 in. (30 cm) long. Weave them together to make a "mat" of 18 x 24 strips. As you weave, keep the strips as straight as possible. Lay the woven "mat" facedown to adjust and tighten up when you have finished.

2 Using the template on page 164, cut a piece of self-adhesive mountboard for the front of the frame. Peel off the backing and stick onto the back of the woven paper, lining up the strips with the apertures.

3 Place the frame facedown and stick double-sided tape along all the edges. One by one, carefully cut the strips away where they cross the apertures, leaving approximately ⅜ in. (1 cm) to turn over and fix to the tape.

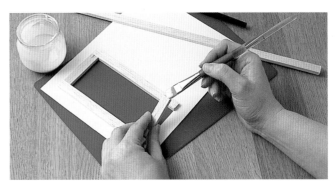

4 Use the same template to cut the backing for your frame from the white mountboard. Follow line B to cut the aperture. Cut four lengths of balsa wood to fit the aperture, as shown, and stick in position with PVA glue.

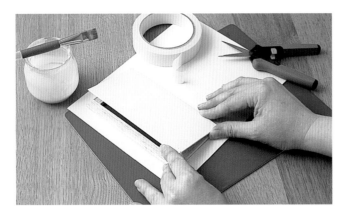

5 Take the piece of mountboard that has been cut out to make the aperture and, using PVA glue, stick this on top of the balsa wood. Use masking tape as an extra fixative to ensure a tight seal.

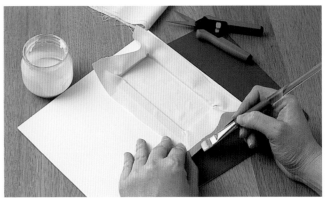

6 Turn the board over and line the recess with a piece of fabric. Brush on a thin smear of PVA glue to fix the fabric in position, wrapping it over the edges.

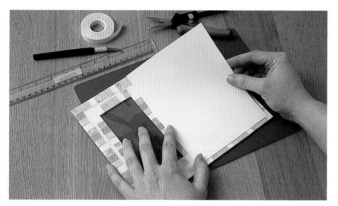

7 Place the front of the frame facedown and use double-sided tape to stick a sheet of acetate to it. Tape your chosen picture in the larger aperture.

8 Place double-sided tape all around the edges of the frame, as shown. Glue your mementoes in the recess and stick the frame together.

9 Take a 7⅗ x 4-in. (19.5 x 10-cm) piece of white mountboard. Cut through half the depth of the board 1½ in. (4 cm) from the top and bend it.

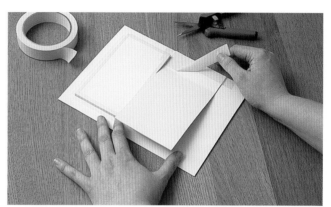

10 Smear PVA glue over the smaller area and stick this facedown on the back of the frame as shown. Add some masking tape across the top for additional strength.

11 Finish the frame by adding some corner embellishments to the front.

CRAFTER'S TIP

For the wedding frame shown on page 37, the same technique has been used but with different measurements and orientation. The recess was lined with a silk remnant from the wedding dress and dried flowers from the bouquet were placed inside. A tiny envelope made from vellum was attached to hold wedding rice.

Scented mobile

A scented mobile is an excellent way to fragrance a room. First create your own unique scented paper using essential oil and dried petals from your garden. Then make up this decorative mobile complete with tassels, filling it with the potpourri of your choice. Alternatively, you could use bought paper to great effect.

TECHNIQUE: Papermaking and piercing **LEVEL:** Intermediate **TIME:** 6 hours

MATERIALS NEEDED:

- Papermaking equipment (see page 16)
- Masking tape
- Cotton linter
- Essential oil
- Dried petals
- Purple dye
- Ultrafine glitter
- Sequins
- Glitter thread
- Felt mat
- Single-needle tool
- Narrow double-sided tape
- Transparent thread
- Beads
- Potpourri
- Electrical wire or coat hanger
- Wire cutters and pliers

For the bunny mobile:

- Cream card
- Light green and yellow flannel paper
- Cotton wool
- PVA glue

1 Following the instructions for "Wedding Stationery" on pages 114 to117, use masking tape to make handmade paper diamond shapes from cotton linter. Scent the vat with your chosen essential oil. Instead of using silk to decorate your paper, as in Step 5 of the "Wedding Stationery" project, use petals, drops of purple dye, and ultrafine glitter.

2 When the paper is dry, take 12 diamonds and sew on sequins with glitter thread.

3 Lay each diamond on the felt pad and use the single-needle tool to prick spiral patterns through the paper.

4 To make the diamond pockets, stick double-sided tape on the reverse side of the bottom two-thirds of six shapes.

5 Stick the remaining six diamonds on top, back to back, and using a large running stitch, sew the bottom two-thirds to strengthen the pocket.

6 Attach a tassel of glitter thread and beads to the bottom of each diamond pocket.

7 Fill each pocket with potpourri and attach a length of beaded thread to the top.

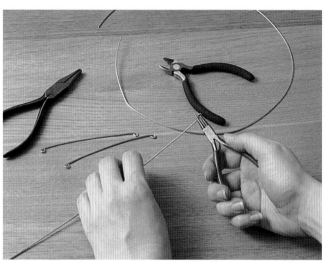

8 Cut one 12-in. (30-cm) and two 5-in. (12.5-cm) lengths of wire and curl all the ends over.

9 Attach the diamonds at varying lengths to the wires with the beaded thread, as shown.

10 Adjust the position of the threads along the wires to balance the mobile; then secure them in position with a dab of PVA glue.

In this variation a card template is covered with flannel paper, and essential oil is dropped onto the bunnies' tails.

11 **TO MAKE THE CHILDREN'S BUNNY MOBILE:** Using the template on page 164, cut out six bunnies in cream card. Stick them on the back of the flannel paper, and cut them out.

12 Stick more flannel paper to the other side of the bunnies, sandwiching the end of a length of transparent thread at the top before recutting.

13 For the tails, stick small balls of cotton wool at the base with PVA glue. Let dry before scenting with a suitable essential oil.

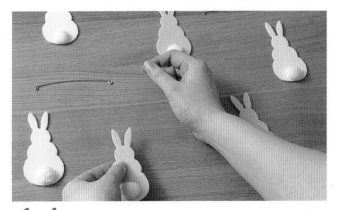

14 Follow Steps 8 to 10 to complete the mobile, adjusting the position of the threads to balance the mobile when hanging.

CRAFTER'S TIP

Lavender oil is a great aid to restful sleep. Saturate the bunnies' tails with lavender essential oil and hang it beside a child's bed, or fill the diamonds with dried lavender and hang them in a bedroom window to enjoy the beneficial properties of this herb.

Everlasting paper flowers

Bring a touch of summer meadows into your home with these delicate flowers made from tissue and crepe paper. Both papers are inexpensive and readily available in an extensive range of colors. Once you have mastered this project, you can fill your house with everlasting bouquets.

TECHNIQUE: Paper cutting **LEVEL:** Intermediate **TIME:** 4–5 hours (to make a vaseful)

MATERIALS NEEDED:
- Red, black, light green, and dark green tissue paper
- Brown crepe paper
- Floral wire stems
- Fine green wire
- Green floristry tape
- Scissors

1 For each poppy, cut three 1½-in. (4-cm) circles of brown crepe paper, one 3-in. (7.5-cm) circle of black tissue. Using the templates on page 164, cut two red petal shapes and two leaves, one in light-green tissue and one in dark-green.

2 Make a small hook at one end of a floral wire stem and bury this in the middle of two brown crepe circles. Crush the paper around the wire into a small ball.

3 Cover the ball with a third brown crepe circle and secure in place with fine green wire. Snip off the end of the wire.

4 Fold a circle of black tissue into quarters and make fine ½-in (13-mm) cuts all around the curved edge. Open out and thread the wire stem through the center. Gather evenly around the crepe ball and secure with fine wire.

5 Make several vertical crease lines in two red petal shapes and thread them through the centers onto the wire stem. Gather up around the base of the center and secure with fine wire. Crease further to create a natural shape.

6 Wrap green floristry tape around the base of the flower and continue down the stem, using the tape to secure two green leaves partway down the stem.

Floral frame

This project shows how easy it is to create a personal gift or keepsake for treasured family photographs. There is no need to try to find a frame of the right size when, with just a few paper napkins and some mountboard, you can make your own beautiful frame to fit your photograph perfectly.

TECHNIQUE: Napkin decoupage **LEVEL:** Intermediate **TIME:** 2–3 hours

MATERIALS NEEDED:

- White and colored mountboard
- 3-ply paper napkin with a floral pattern
- Decoupage glue and foam brush
- Herbal fruit tea bag and a little warm water
- Ribbons
- Double-sided tape
- Sticky tape
- Cutting mat, ruler, pencil, and craft knife

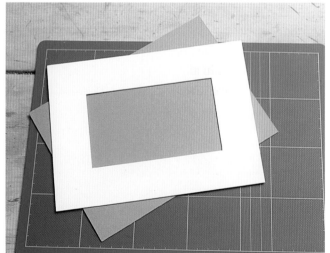

1 Measure the height and width of the photo you would like to frame. Add 2¾ in. (7 cm) to each of these measurements. Cut out two pieces of white mountboard to this size, plus two pieces in color.

2 Cut the aperture for the photo in one of the white pieces. Lay the second white piece on top of a colored piece. Cut in half along the long edge to form the two front flaps.

3 Remove the two backing pieces of tissue from the napkin and discard. Lay the top, patterned layer over the white frame and cut roughly to size. Repeat for the two white flaps.

4 Spread the decoupage glue over the surface of the frame and gently pat the napkin into position. Repeat with the two flaps of the frame.

CRAFTER'S TIP

Instead of having one large photo, you can cut several apertures in the frame, as well as on the inside of the flaps, to display a series of photos.

5 Cut the corners off the napkins from all three pieces. Cut and remove the napkin from the center of the frame, leaving an excess of ½ in. (13 mm). Snip into the corners of the window.

6 Using the foam brush and decoupage glue, fold over and stick down the excess napkin. Spread more glue over the napkin on both the frame and the flaps. Leave to dry.

7 Soak the tea bag in warm water for a couple of minutes, then squeeze out the excess. Use the tea bag to sponge the colored mountboard; then let dry.

Follow the floral theme for a group of family photos.

8 Using a pencil and ruler, mark the position for the ribbon hinges and the ribbon tie on the reverse side of the colored mountboard. Stick the ribbon in position with tape.

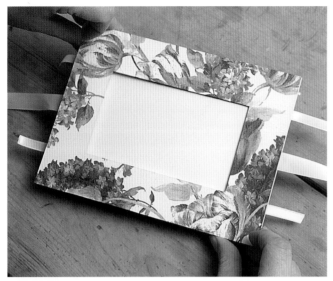

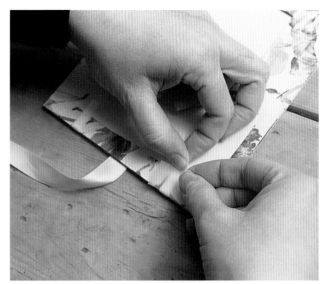

9 Stick double-sided tape down each side and along the bottom of the back piece. Position the front of the frame on top and press into place.

10 Place the front flap facedown on top of the frame and stick the ribbon hinges in place with tape.

11 Stick double-sided tape around the edges of the flaps and position the back of the flaps on top. Press them into place.

12 Slide your chosen photograph into the frame through the top opening.

CRAFTER'S TIP

To make sure the finished frame fits together well, measure and cut the first piece of mountboard; then use this as a template for cutting out the other pieces. This is especially important when cutting the pieces in half to form the flaps.

Gilded mirror frame

Everyone knows you can use gilding waxes on wood, but they are also very effective on card. Here a simple wooden frame has been transformed with an embossed card lightly gilded with gold wax. Practice gilding first on scrap card to avoid applying too much wax.

TECHNIQUE: Embossing **LEVEL:** Intermediate **TIME:** 3 hours

MATERIALS NEEDED:

- Dark green card
- Embossing system with "lizard" stencil
- Clear wax candle
- Gold gilding wax
- Small gold brads
- Double-sided tape
- Masking tape
- Pencil
- Wooden frame
- Mirror to fit frame
- Craft knife, cutting mat, and ruler

1 Use the wooden frame as a template for cutting the green card to fit; then cut this into quarters. Cut four squares the width of the frame. Measure in ⅜ in. (1 cm) from two adjacent corners and trim, as shown.

2 Rub the back of each frame corner with a wax candle before placing the pieces of waxed card facedown on the embossing system. Emboss the whole lizard pattern. On each of the small pieces, emboss a lizard facing the wider edge.

3 Use gilding wax to turn the outer and inner edges of the wooden frame gold. Apply a very small amount of wax with your finger, as shown, to gild the embossed pieces of card.

4 Lay the card frame on the wooden one and stick the pieces together using strips of double-sided tape.

5 Remove the backing from the tape to stick the small pieces over the joins and, using a craft knife, make small diagonal slits at each corner to add the brads.

6 Use more double-sided tape around the inner and outer edges of the card to stick it to the wooden frame. Insert the mirror glass and secure with masking tape on the back.

CRAFTER'S TIP

With a pencil, lightly mark up each corner of both the card and wooden frame on the reverse side to make it easier to reassemble.

Decoupaged clock

This attractive three-dimensional design turns a mundane object into a work of art smart enough to grace any wall. Three-dimensional decoupage produces great results. It can be a little time-consuming, especially if you have chosen a design that requires intricate cutting, but your patience will always be rewarded.

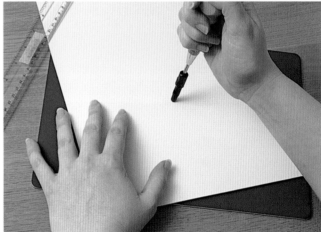

1 Cut a 9½ x 16⅖-in. (24 x 42-cm) piece of mountboard. Using an eyeletting punch, make a hole in the center 4¾ in. (12 cm) from one short edge.

2 Using scissors, a craft knife, and a mat, cut out four or five layers of the decoupage print. Remember that the back layer always remains uncut, while each progressive layer features fewer items, graduating forward until only a few flowers remain.

TECHNIQUE: 3-D decoupage **LEVEL:** Intermediate **TIME:** 4–5 hours

MATERIALS NEEDED:

- Mountboard
- Five or six 8 x 5⁷⁄₈-in. (20 x 15-cm) 3-D identical decoupage prints
- Clock mechanism and hands
- Scissors
- Silicone glue
- Acid-free adhesive
- Die-cut templates, numbered 0–9
- Die-cut machine
- Protractor
- Eyeletting punch
- 4 metal book corners
- Craft knife, cutting mat, and ruler

3 Use adhesive to stick the background print at the bottom of the mountboard, leaving an even border. Cut five flowers from the remnants and stick these around the punched hole at the top of the mountboard.

4 Cut two triangles from the background of the decoupage print remnants and fix them in the top corners. Punch numbers using the die-cut templates. With the aid of a protractor, stick these in a circle 3 in. (7.5 cm) from the hole.

5 Use silicone glue to fix the decoupage layers in position on top of the background layer at the bottom of the mountboard.

6 Leave to dry before fixing the clock mechanism in position, as shown. Fix protective metal embellishments to each corner.

Festive lights

Everybody likes to make something different for a party, whether it be for Christmas, a birthday, or any special occasion. Why not create these delightful fairy light shades? They are quick and easy to make, and there is no limit to the scope for variation with so many lovely papers from which to choose.

TECHNIQUES: Collage and laminating **LEVEL:** Beginner **TIME:** 2–3 hours

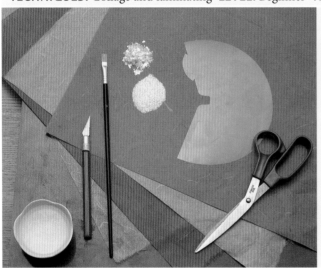

MATERIALS NEEDED:
- Lime-green, yellow, pink, and orange mulberry paper
- Pencil and ruler
- Brush and water
- Transparent, glossy laminating fairy light shades
- Cotton cloth or tea towel
- Iron and hard heat-resistant surface
- Ultrafine iridescent glitter
- Iridescent pearl flakes
- Cutting mat, craft knife, and scissors

1 Using the pencil and ruler, draw ten 3½-in. (9-cm) squares on each color of mulberry paper. To make the fluffy edges, wet the paper along the pencil lines using the brush, and gently pull apart.

2 Lay the cotton cloth on the heat-resistant surface and place the laminating shade on top, glossy side down. Sprinkle some iridescent pearl flakes and ultrafine glitter randomly over the surface.

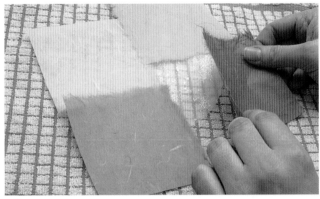

3 Cover the shade with four different-colored squares of paper, placed edge to edge. Cover with the cotton cloth and iron to fix the papers to the shade, following the manufacturer's instructions.

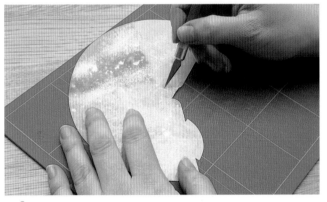

4 Using scissors and a craft knife, where necessary, carefully cut away the excess paper and open the slot for the tab fixing of the shade.

CRAFTER'S TIP

For an alternative look, use pretty paper napkins or rubber-stamped papers to decorate your fairy light shades.

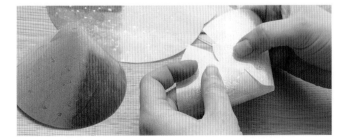

5 Carefully fold each shade into a cone shape, fastening around the fairy lights and push the tabs into the slots.

Vacation scrapbook pages

Scrapbooking has turned photo albums into works of art and not just somewhere to store your favorite photos. Here are a couple of novel layering or matting ideas. The first, using concertina folds, allows you to add as many photos as you like in the space of just one photo, while the second creates a secret hiding place using memorabilia from your vacation. The concertina photos work best with an odd number of photos.

TECHNIQUE: Scrapbooking **LEVEL:** Intermediate **TIME:** 2–3 hours

MATERIALS NEEDED:

- Photos
- Plain card
- Decorative card
- Eyelet-setting tools
- Brad and eyelets
- Decorative fiber
- Metal clips
- Cookie or candy wrappers
- Vellum
- Scissors
- Acid-free dry adhesive and double-sided tape
- Craft knife, cutting mat, and ruler

1 **TO MAKE THE CONCERTINA PHOTOS:** Mat the photos on plain card and trim to a ⅛-in. (3-mm) border before matting them on decorative card trimmed to a ¼-in. (6-mm) border.

2 Use eyelet tools to make two holes in the backing card at the top and bottom of each photo and attach eyelets. Join the photos together by threading fibers through the adjoining sides.

3 Attach a metal clip in the middle of a length of fiber. Thread this fiber through the top two eyelets, leaving a loop in the middle with approximately 4 in. (10 cm) at either end. Tie knots to hold in position.

4 Attach metal clips at either end of the fiber before sticking the base photo to the page. Fix the middle clip with a little stitch through the background sheet to hold it in place.

5 **TO MAKE THE HIDDEN PHOTO:** Using dry adhesive, fix a cookie or candy wrapper to a sheet of vellum and trim. Stick the photo in the center. Fold over the edges and cut away the corners.

6 Fix a brad to the bottom flap and fix an eyelet in the top flap. Fold the flaps over and, before fixing to the page, thread a short length of fiber through the eyelet to keep it closed.

CRAFTER'S TIP

A pH-detector pen allows you to check the acidity of paper. If something isn't acid-free, it will deteriorate over time.

Quilled coasters

Quilling is the art of creating pictures from rolled coils of paper strips. The designs can be either intricate or simple, and they can be used to decorate any manner of items, including the coasters shown here. If you enjoy parchment craft, you may well like quilling too, so why not try your hand at these gerbera and dahlia designs?

MATERIALS NEEDED:

- 1 small and 1 large glass coaster
- ⅛-in. (3-mm) quilling strips in deep pink, green, orange, and yellow
- Quilling tool
- Quilling boards
- Toothpicks

- PVA glue
- Tweezers
- Pins
- Decorating chalks
- Sticky-backed cork
- Scissors
- Rule

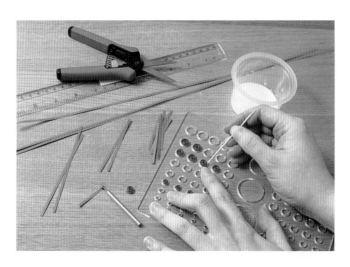

1 For the dahlia, cut the following approximate lengths of deep pink paper strips and, keeping the edges even, use a quilling tool to roll them into circles: six 2-in. (5-cm) strips for center petals—makes ¼-in. (6-mm) circles; ten 4-in. (10-cm) strips for large petals—makes ⅖-in. (10-mm) circles; ten 3-in. (7.5-cm) strips for medium petals—makes ⅜-in. (9-mm) circles; twenty 2-in. (5-cm) strips for small petals—makes ¼-in. (6-mm) circles. Place the circles in the appropriate-sized holes in the quilling board. Secure the ends with a dab of PVA glue applied with a toothpick.

2 When dry, hold each circle with the glued end facing you. Squeeze the circle between the thumb and forefinger of one hand and pinch the end to a point to make a petal shape. For the center petals, flatten the other end to make a more triangular shape.

3 On the quilling board, stick the six center petals together with glue to form the dahlia center, holding it in position with pins.

4 Assemble the dahlia by sticking the large petals around the center with the medium petals in between and the smaller petals on either side.

5 Using green decorating chalks, lightly color a ⅖-in. (10-mm) edge around the base card of the small coaster and stick the completed dahlia to the center.

6 Cut nine 2-in. (5-cm) green paper strips. Make scrolls by loosely rolling one end almost to the center; then turn it over and roll the other end almost to the center.

7 Squeeze the ends of the scrolls and glue these around the dahlia.

8 Using the coaster as a guide, cut a hole in the sticky-backed cork. Position the hole over the base of the coaster and trim the excess cork with scissors. This will give the necessary depth for the quilling.

9 Assemble the coaster by inserting the quilled decoration and sticking the green baize backing onto the base of the insert.

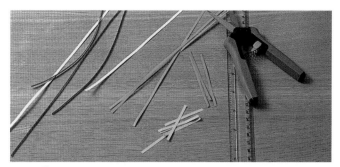

CRAFTER'S TIP

While a quilling tool and board make it easier to make identical coils, you can use a toothpick (or cocktail stick) and felt pad covered with waxed paper. To achieve even coils, make sure that your strips are the same length.

10 For the gerbera, cut the following approximate lengths of paper strips: one 9-in. (23-cm) yellow strip for the center; one 18-in. (46-cm) orange strip for the center; fourteen 9-in. (23-cm) orange strips for the large petals; fourteen 3-in. (7.5-cm) orange strips for the small petals; twelve 2-in. (5-cm) green strips for the scrolls.

11 Stick the strips for the center together with PVA glue to form a single strip. Starting at the yellow end, roll the strip into a ⅗-in. (15-mm) circle, securing the end with PVA glue. Pin this completed circle to the quilling board.

12 As with the dahlia, roll the strips for the petals into ⅗-in. (15-mm) circles using the 9-in. (23-cm) strips and 5⁄16-in. (8-mm) circles with the 3-in. (7.5-cm) strips. Secure the loose ends with PVA glue and let dry.

13 To create the petals, hold each large circle at the glued end and, with the other hand, squeeze the circle. Then carefully flatten the glued end. Repeat for the small circles, but squeeze the end to a point. Use PVA glue to stick the large petals around the center with the smaller petals in between.

14 Follow Steps 5 to 9 to make up the gerbera coaster, but make 12 green scrolls instead of nine and do not flatten them.

Summer lantern

Add a touch of fairy magic to leisurely summer evenings in the garden with these delicate paper lanterns, decorated with funky thread and tiny metallic bells. Suspended over a string of outdoor lights, they will delight with their soft, tinkling music as they gently sway in the cool summer breeze.

TECHNIQUE: Patchwork **LEVEL:** Advanced **TIME:** 4–5 hours

MATERIALS NEEDED:

- Heavyweight wet-strength tissue paper
- Microwave and microwavable dish
- Vinegar, water, and dropper
- Microwavable pink and purple fabric dyes
- Iron, soft cloth, and ironing board
- Self-adhesive mountboard
- Lilac mulberry paper
- Revolving punch plier
- Eyeletting hole punch
- ¼-in. (6-mm) doweling, craft saw, and sandpaper
- PVA glue and brush
- Spangles and metallic bells
- Decorative pink funky fur thread (use extra as optional trim)
- Cutting mat, ruler, and craft knife

1 To make the decorative paper to create your lantern, scrunch some wet-strength tissue paper in a microwavable dish. Using a dropper, wet the paper with a mixture of equal parts water and vinegar.

2 Drop pink and purple fabric dyes over the surface of the tissue paper. For a delicate, variegated look, use the dyes both undiluted and watered down.

3 Place in the microwave and heat. Be sure to follow the dye manufacturer's instructions. When fixed, take the paper out and iron it flat between two soft cloths.

4 Enlarge the templates on page 169, and use to cut the top and bottom of the lantern from the self-adhesive mountboard.

5 Following the positions marked on the template, use the revolving punch to make the holes for the dowels and the eyeletting punch to make the smaller holes for the handle and tassel.

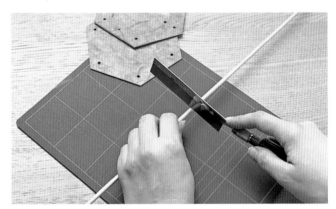

6 Peel back the protective layers from the mountboard and lay them facedown on the lilac mulberry paper. Trim away the excess with a craft knife and repunch the holes.

7 Cut six 7½-in. (19-cm) lengths of ¼-in. (6-mm) doweling and sand any rough edges.

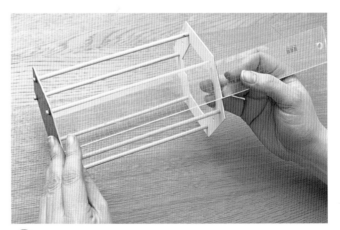

8 Carefully push the dowels through the holes to connect the top and bottom to make the lantern structure.

9 Make sure the dowels are evenly positioned, leaving 7 in. (18 cm) between the top and bottom of the lantern.

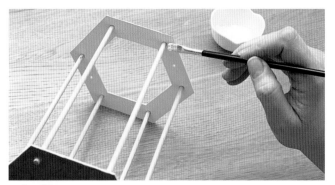

10 Fix the dowels in position by brushing them with PVA glue where they meet the mountboard. Leave to dry.

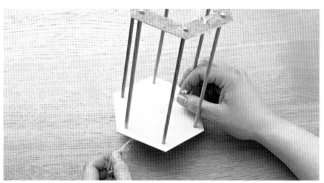

11 Cut lengths of thread for the handle and as an anchor for the tassel. Thread them through the holes, tie knots in the ends, and fix with PVA glue.

12 Using a craft knife and ruler, cut three pieces of tissue paper 2¾ x 7 in. (7 x 18 cm) and three pieces 2⅜ x 7 in. (6 x 18 cm). Brush glue onto two adjoining struts. Stick one large piece of tissue across the gap, wrapping the ends around the glued struts to secure.

13 Repeat with the other two large pieces of tissue across the four uncovered struts. Apply more glue to the tissue-covered struts and stick the smaller pieces of tissue across the gaps to enclose the lantern.

14 Thread bells and spangles onto more threads and attach to the tassel anchor. As an option, thread more bells onto the fur thread. Knot the thread around the bottom of one strut. You could then wrap the fur around the base a few times before working your way up and down the lantern and tying off.

CRAFTER'S TIP

You could use night-lights inside the lanterns rather than hanging them over garden lights. Spray your paper and dowels with flame-retardant spray and make sure you use a small glass container for your night-light.

3-D Christmas decorations

Vellums are available in many colors and designs, and are ideal for making a tree decoration, like the one shown above, that can be filled with popcorn. Alternatively, you could try kirigami, the art of paper folding and cutting, to make different-colored metallic-paper stars (opposite).

TECHNIQUES: Kirigami and parchment craft **LEVEL:** Advanced **TIME:** 3–4 hours

MATERIALS NEEDED

For the vellum bags:
- Vellum
- Masking tape and double-sided tape
- 3-D paint
- Ultrafine glitter
- Single-needle tool, 4-needle tool, and heart-needle tool
- Felt pad
- Metallic threads and brads

For the kirigami stars:
- 5-in. (13-cm) square of metallic origami paper
- Eyelet punch
- 3-D paint and ultrafine glitter
- Sticky tape
- Metallic thread
- Craft knife, cutting mat, and ruler

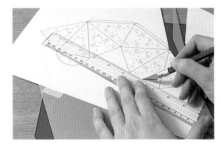

1 **TO MAKE THE VELLUM DECORATIONS:** Enlarge the template on page 166, cut out and score the vellum.

2 Lightly tape the template to the vellum. Lay them on the felt pad and use parchment tools to prick out the design.

3 Apply dots of 3-D paint and sprinkle with ultrafine glitter. Let dry, then brush off the excess. Fix a brad in position.

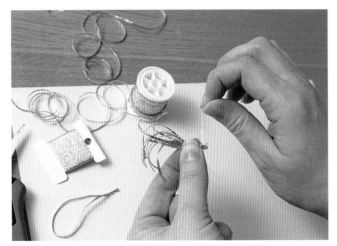

4 Cut six 5-in. (13-cm) lengths of thread, lay them together, and tie another piece of thread around their center. Fold the lengths in half. Wrap the center thread around the end, then tie off to create a tassel.

5 Cut an 8-in. (20.5-cm) length of metallic thread and tie it in a loop. Cut off the top point of the vellum decoration and stick the top half together with double-sided tape, encapsulating the knot of the loop.

6 Trim the tassel and use a single-needle tool to fluff it out. Cut the bottom point off and again use double-sided tape to stick the sides together, encapsulating the top of the tassel.

7 Knot the end of a short piece of thread and feed it through the hole in the flap. Wind it around the brad to keep the decoration closed.

CRAFTER'S TIP

You will achieve better results with kirigami if you use a thin paper, such as origami paper; and for an even design, make sure your folds are accurate.

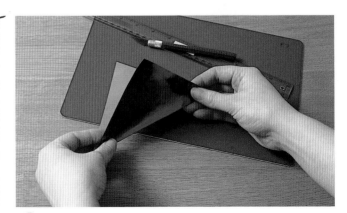

8 **TO MAKE THE KIRIGAMI STARS:** Fold the square of metallic origami paper in half.

9 Follow the template on page 165 to fold the right point over and then fold it back on itself.

10 Turn the paper over and repeat the folds so that the other side lines up with the edges.

11 Follow the template to cut and punch out shapes using a craft knife and eyelet punch.

12 Open out the design, turning some folds so that the points are all mountain folds.

13 Repeat Steps 8 to 12 with a matching piece of paper and decorate with 3-D paint and ultrafine glitter before leaving to dry.

14 Use small pieces of tape to join the two stars and cover the join with 3-D paint. Thread a length of fiber through holes near the tip of one point.

Christmas scrapbook pages

With a couple of tissues, a little PVA glue, and a rubber stamp, you can make your own embossed paper embellishments. If you're new to sewing paper, then you'll have fun making this snowflake picture frame. The hardest part is designing your snowflake, but persevere and you'll have a scrapbook page that is sure to impress.

TECHNIQUES: Scrapbooking and paper casting **LEVEL:** Advanced **TIME:** 3–4 hours

MATERIALS NEEDED:

- 3-ply men's paper tissues
- Snowflake stamp
- Paintbrush and water
- Acid-free adhesive
- Plastic pocket
- Pearly powders
- Scissors
- Tracing paper
- Protractor
- Pencil
- Single-needle tool
- Glittery thread and needle
- Acid-free double-sided tape
- Rule

1 TO MAKE THE STAMP PAPER CAST: Cut eight squares of tissue large enough to cover the stamp. Using a brush and mixture of acid-free adhesive and water, apply a square to the stamp, carefully pushing it into the recesses with the brush. While still wet, apply another seven squares individually on top of the first. Set aside for 10 minutes.

2 Carefully remove the square from the stamp. Let dry on the plastic pocket.

3 Using your fingertips, apply pearly powders over the top of the square. Trim the edges before fixing to the scrapbook page.

4 TO MAKE THE SNOW-FLAKE PHOTO HOLDER: Draw around your chosen photo onto tracing paper. Find the center point and, using a protractor as an aid, draw a snowflake pattern on the tracing paper, making sure that an arm goes across each corner of the outline of the photo.

5 Position the tracing over your page. Prick each intersection point with a single-needle tool.

6 Use a needle to sew the glittery thread through the holes to create the snowflake, tying off the ends on the reverse. Stick a small piece of double-sided acid-free tape in the center on the reverse of the photo to fix it in position, tucking the corners under the threads.

Children's Accessories

Children are forever changing their minds as they grow and develop. One minute purple is their favorite color and next it is green, or one day they love wild animals, and then it's nothing but sports that grabs their attention. Trying to keep up with their likes and dislikes can prove rather expensive when it comes to decorating their rooms. Within this chapter you will discover that it can be fun and inexpensive updating your children's room accessories as their likes and dislikes evolve. Use the ideas provided here, such as the lamp shade, bookends, toy box, and mobile, and theme them to suit your child.

Night-light

All you need is a piece of vellum and some colored card to create
this simple but effective night-light, which is just the thing to help children drift off to
sleep. A die-cut machine has been used to create the butterflies and flowers, but you can
cut out your own shapes with scissors or a craft knife, if you prefer.

TECHNIQUES: Paper piercing and collage **LEVEL:** Beginner **TIME:** 2–3 hours

MATERIALS NEEDED:

- Blue vellum
- Assorted pastel-colored card
- Die-cut machine with butterfly and flower templates
- Dry adhesive
- Single-needle tool
- Felt pad
- Double-sided tape
- Column lamp with low-watt bulb
- Craft knife, cutting mat, and ruler

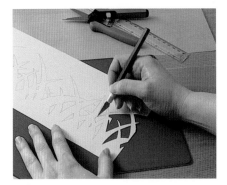

1 Cut a 9¼ x 17¾-in. (23 x 45-cm) piece of blue vellum. Enlarge the template on page 168 and use to cut the grass from the pastel green card with a craft knife.

2 Using a die-cut machine, cut out butterflies and flowers from pastel-colored card. Vary the colors in the different sections of the butterflies.

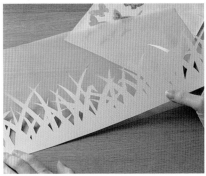

3 Apply dry adhesive to the backs of the grass, butterflies, and flowers. Stick the grass to the bottom of the vellum.

4 Still attached to the adhesive backing sheet, lay the flowers and butterflies over the felt pad and make tiny holes with the needle tool. Stick the flowers and butterflies above the grass in a random fashion.

5 Cut a small square from the bottom edge 1 in. (2.5 cm) from one end. (This is for the electric cord.)

6 Using double-sided tape, secure the two ends of the decorated vellum together to form a tube. Make sure the edges match exactly.

Decorated box

Here is a cleverly disguised box that not only fulfills its practical function of hiding unused toys but also adds a fun element to storage. Any child would delight in having this bright and cheerful box in his or her room.

TECHNIQUE: Paper layering **LEVEL:** Beginner **TIME:** 4–5 hours

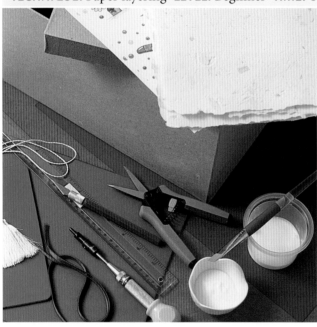

MATERIALS NEEDED:

- 12-in. (30-cm)-square papier-mâché box
- Handmade paper with sawdust inclusions (see pages 16–18)
- Purple, white, and red card
- Paper, for lining box
- Ivory acrylic paint
- Clown prints
- Eyelet punch
- Corded tassel with 3-in. (7.5-cm) cord
- Red ribbon
- Double-sided tape
- Brush
- PVA and dry adhesives
- Craft knife, cutting mat, and ruler

1 Use PVA glue to stick handmade paper on each side of the box, wrapping the paper ¼ in. (6 mm) over the top edge. Stick 3⅛-in. (8-cm) strips of purple paper around each corner. Cover the edges of the lid in the same way.

2 Line the inside of the box with more paper, using the technique described in Steps 3–4 on page 122, and paint the inside of the lid. Leave to dry. Cut out eight clowns and stick two on each side of the box.

3 Using an eyelet punch, make a hole in the center of the lid. Thread a tassel with a 3-in. (7.5-cm) cord up through the hole. Tie this to a loop made from a 19-in. (48-cm) length of red ribbon.

4 Enlarge the triangular template on page 166 and use it to cut and score four pieces of white card and two pieces of red card. It is easier to cut around the semicircles with scissors. To make the two-tone effect, cut the red card into strips and, using dry adhesive, stick alternate strips on the white card.

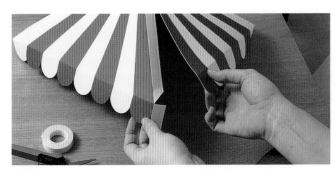

5 Assemble the roof with double-sided tape along each flap.

6 Thread the loop of ribbon up through the center hole in the roof before sticking the scalloped edge to the sides of the box lid.

Cat-and-dog lamp shade

Most children's bedrooms have a theme, whether it be animals, sports, or fairies. Here's an easy way to create a lamp shade to match. You don't even need to buy a frame, since you can recycle an old one by using the technique described on page 33 to make the pattern for the shade.

TECHNIQUE: Stamping **LEVEL:** Beginner **TIME:** 3–4 hours

MATERIALS NEEDED:

- Cream card
- Chestnut and barn-brown ink pads
- Dog, cat, and paw-print stamps
- Acid-free baby wipes or stamp cleaner
- Watercolor pencils and brush

- Double-sided tape
- PVA glue
- 5-in. (13-cm)-diameter lamp-shade wire frame
- Cream bias binding tape
- Craft knife, cutting mat, and ruler

1 Cut the lamp shade shape from the card, using the template on page 166. Place the dog stamp upside down on your work surface and lightly pat it with the chestnut ink pad until you have even coverage.

2 With a steady, positive motion, press the stamp onto the card. Holding it with one hand, walk the fingers of your other hand over the stamp. Remove the stamp and clean with a baby wipe or stamp cleaner.

3 Lightly color in the darker areas of the dog with watercolor pencils and use a wet brush to spread the color through the rest of the image.

4 Using the chestnut pad for the dog and the barn-brown pad for the cat, continue stamping cats and dogs in the curves around the bottom edge of the shade. Stamp an undulating line of paw prints, using the chestnut pad, around the upper half of the shade.

5 Color the cats and dogs with watercolor pencils, as in Step 3. Use the barn-brown ink pad to carefully apply ink directly around the bottom edge of the lamp shade.

6 Using PVA glue, stick one-half of the bias binding around the top edge of the lamp shade. Snip the overlap of the bias binding to even out the join. Close up the shade using double-sided tape along one edge. Apply glue to the exposed half of the binding and fold over the wire frame to fix.

Bookends

With bold, graphic shapes these stenciled bookends are sure to be admired by older children who will delight in storing their favorite tales of knights, dragons, and damsels in distress in between.

TECHNIQUE: Stenciling **LEVEL:** Intermediate **TIME:** 5–6 hours

MATERIALS NEEDED:

- Masking tape
- Acetate
- Stencil cutter and piece of glass (optional)
- Mountboard
- Stencil sponges and brushes
- Acrylic paints and palette
- Card remnant
- Basswood or balsa-wood strips
- Craft saw
- Sandpaper
- All-purpose glue or balsa cement
- Stones or pebbles
- Craft knife, cutting mat, and ruler

Princess variation:
- Fine wire mesh
- Fragrant beads, glass pebbles, and shells—in place of stones or pebbles

1 To make your stencil, use masking tape to temporarily fix the knight template from page 167 facedown on a piece of glass. Turn it over and fix a sheet of acetate on the other side before tracing around the design with a heated stencil cutter. Repeat for the dragon. (You can use a craft knife and cutting mat, but this will take longer and is more difficult.)

2 Use the outer line on the templates to cut a piece of mountboard for the knight and another for the dragon. Place the mountboard cutouts facedown on another piece of mountboard. Carefully trace around them with a pencil and then cut them out for the second bookend.

3 Use masking tape to temporarily fix your stencils to the mountboard shapes. Using a stencil sponge or brush, apply acrylic paints to each area. Use a small piece of card to protect adjacent areas while painting. Clean your stencils after each use and remember to flip them over for the second bookend. Leave to dry.

4 For each bookend, cut two side panels 4 x 3 in. (10 x 7.5 cm) and two panels for the base and lid 3 x 5⅞ in. (7.5 x 15 cm) from mountboard. Use a modeling or craft saw to cut two 5⅛-in. (13-cm), two 2¼-in. (6-cm), and four 3⁷⁄₁₆-in. (9-cm) lengths from the basswood or balsa wood. (Balsa wood is easier to cut, but basswood is stronger.)

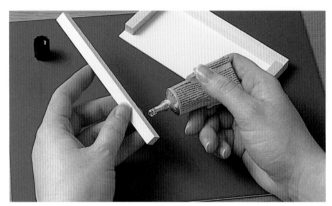

5 Take the base and, with balsa cement or all-purpose glue, stick the 5⅛-in. (13-cm) and 2¼-in. (6-cm) lengths neatly around the edges. Hold them together for a minute or two until they are firmly stuck in place.

6 Stick a side panel in place, followed by two 3⁷⁄₁₆-in. (9-cm) struts, holding them in position for a minute while the glue hardens.

7 Attach the front panel of the stenciled design, making sure that the sides line up with the edge.

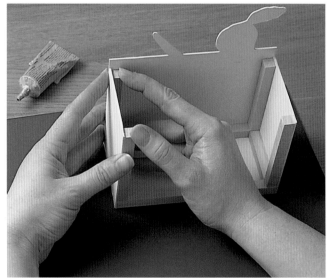

8 When the glue has hardened, stick the second side panel in place, followed by the last two struts.

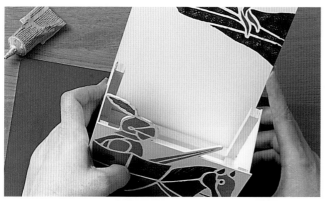

9 Finally, stick the back panel in position, lining up the edges and remembering to wait for the glue to harden. Repeat Steps 5 to 9 for the second bookend.

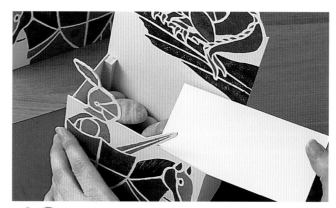

10 Fill both boxes with pebbles to weight them down. Make sure that your lid fits, trimming if necessary. Add a dab of glue to the top of each balsa strut and stick the lid in place.

11 **TO MAKE THE PRINCESS BOOKEND:** Cut a 1½ x 2½-in. (4 x 6-cm) aperture in each side panel and stick a 2 x 3-in. (5 x 7.5-cm) piece of wire mesh to the back of each before making up.

12 Fill these boxes with lavender-scented beads to aid peaceful sleep, glass pebbles, and decorative shells.

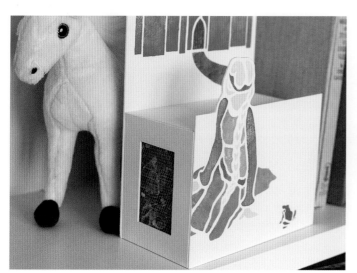

CRAFTER'S TIP

You can mix and match the stencils on page 167. Alternatively, if you'd rather use ready-made stencils, follow the general instructions, adjusting the measurements where appropriate.

Origami mobile

If you have never tried origami before, this project, which uses a traditional Japanese design, is a good way to start. The origami papers are truly exquisite and a joy to work with. What's more, the finished mobile is sure to delight children and will look great hanging in a bedroom.

TECHNIQUE: Origami **LEVEL:** Intermediate **TIME:** 4–5 hours

MATERIALS NEEDED:

- Origami papers (one for each bird)
- White mountboard
- White card
- Blue decorating chalk
- Clear thread
- Parchment needle tool
- Needle
- Scissors
- Double-sided tape or glue
- Craft knife, cutting mat, and ruler

1 Take a 4-in. (10-cm) square of origami paper and fold in half diagonally and then in half again.

2 Lift up the flap, open it out, and squash it flat, as shown. Turn over and repeat on the reverse.

3 With the open end facing downward, lift the bottom point up to the top and press flat. (This is a petal fold.) Turn over and repeat on the reverse.

4 Take one of the bottom points and fold up, as shown. This is for the tail of the bird.

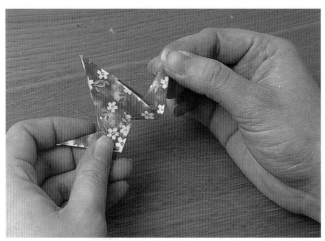

5 Repeat the fold with the other flap to make the neck of the bird.

6 Form the head by folding down a small section of the neck fold, as shown.

7 Take the two upper flaps and fold them down to make the wings.

8 Repeat Steps 1 to 7 with two 6-in. (15-cm) squares and two 4¾-in. (12-cm) squares of origami paper.

9 Enlarge the templates on page 168 and use to cut two large mountboard clouds and two small white card clouds. With a little blue decorating chalk and using your finger, lightly color in patches to give a 3-D effect to the clouds.

10 Following the template guide, make small holes in the mountboard with the needle tool. Thread a piece of clear thread through the hole at the top of one of the large clouds and slot the two pieces together, as shown.

11 Hang the cloud up and, using a needle and more clear thread, attach the origami birds at different heights. Make sure the mobile is balanced before you finish fixing the birds.

12 Stick the two small card clouds back to back above the central bird, sandwiching the thread between them.

CRAFTER'S TIP

Fix the hole centrally to make the bird fly straight. If you want to vary this, remember that the bird's angle of flight depends on where you attach the thread to the bird's back. The closer the hole is to the head, the more the bird will soar upward.

Advent calendar

December is such an exciting month for children, full of anticipation. What better way to mark the countdown to Christmas Day than with your own personalized advent calendar? With just a napkin, some tissue paper, and some glitter, you can create a sparkling calendar to fill with small charms or candies of your choice.

TECHNIQUE: Napkin decoupage **LEVEL:** Intermediate **TIME:** 5–6 hours

MATERIALS NEEDED:

- Advent calendar base with individual compartments
- Paper napkin with a winter scene
- White tissue paper
- Ultrafine iridescent glitter
- Silver peel-off numbers
- Glitter trim
- Mini Christmas stamps
- Black-dye ink pad
- White paper
- Colored pencils
- Blue chalk ink pad
- Candies and charms
- Brush
- Double-sided tape
- Sticky tape
- PVA glue
- Scissors
- Craft knife, cutting mat, and ruler

1 Remove the backing panel from the calendar and put to one side. Use PVA glue to stick the top layer of the napkin to the center of the calendar front and stick torn pieces of white tissue around the edge of the calendar, overlapping the napkin edge.

2 When the glue is dry, trim the tissue to neaten the edges of the calendar. Apply PVA glue to areas of snow on the napkin scene and around the border. Sprinkle on ultrafine glitter and, when dry, brush off the excess.

3 Rescore the window openings with a craft knife and then apply peel-off silver numbers from 1 to 24, either consecutively or at random.

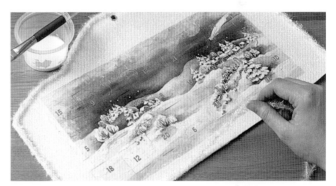

4 Glue the glitter trim around the outside edge of the calendar to finish the front.

5 Cut out 24 x 1⅜-in. (3.5-cm) squares of white paper and then stamp them with mini Christmas images using the black ink pad. Color them in with pencils, and ink the outer edges of each square with the blue chalk pad.

6 Stick the paper squares to larger squares of tissue with double-sided tape. With the image facedown, place candies or charms in the center and wrap up the parcel with a piece of sticky tape. Insert them into the calendar backing before replacing the decorated top.

Book cover 🌸

This customized notebook, with a variety of pockets to hold coordinating stationery items, will delight any child. Quick and simple to make, it would be ideal for writing stories or sketching in during a long trip. Choose your patterned gift wrap according to the child's interests.

TECHNIQUE: Paper cutting and folding **LEVEL:** Beginner **TIME:** 1–2 hours

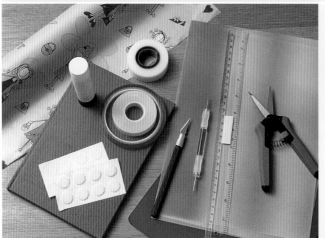

MATERIALS NEEDED:

- Gift wrap
- Blank, handicraft exercise book
- Sticky tape
- Double-sided tape (standard and narrow)
- Colored vellum
- Embossing tool

- Scissors
- Dry glue stick
- Hook-and-loop dots
- Craft knife, cutting mat, and ruler

1 Cover the book with a piece of gift wrap, folding the excess paper over the edges and securing it in position with sticky tape. Use double-sided tape to fix the front and back pages to the covers to hide the excess gift wrap.

2 TO MAKE A STANDARD POCKET: Decide on the size of the pocket and add ½ in. (13 mm) to each side and the bottom. Cut a piece of colored vellum to this size and score a line ½ in. (13 mm) in from the sides and the bottom with an embossing tool. Fold the edges under and miter the bottom corners using scissors.

3 TO MAKE AN EXPANDABLE POCKET: Add 1 in. (2.5 cm) to each side and the bottom of your pocket measurements. Cut a piece of vellum to size and score lines ¼ in. (6 mm), ⅝ in. (16 mm), and 1 in. (26 mm) from the sides and the bottom. Starting with the bottom, fold the edge under along the first score line; then fold up along the second score line and back under again along the third.

4 Repeat the folds for each side and miter the bottom corners, as in Step 2. Stick your pockets to the cover using narrow double-sided tape along the edges.

5 **TO MAKE AN ENVELOPE POCKET:** Begin with an expandable pocket. Cut a piece of vellum slightly narrower than your pocket size but 1 in. (2.5 cm) longer than the height. Score lines 1 in. (2.5 cm), 1⅜ in. (3.5 cm), and 1¾ in. (4.5 cm) down from the top edge. Fold along each line before tucking the short end into the top of your pocket and fixing it in position with double-sided tape.

6 Decorate the pockets with motifs cut from the wrapping paper and stuck on with a dry glue stick. Create a fastening for your envelope pocket by sticking a hook-and-loop dot under the flap and on the pocket, checking that they meet when it is closed. Conceal the hook-and-loop with a motif on the top.

Lion mask

Making a papier-mâché mask using a balloon and old newspapers is a simple technique that can be enjoyed by children and adults alike. Young children will delight in helping you with this project, almost as much as they'll love dressing up and playing with the results!

TECHNIQUE: Papier-mâché **LEVEL:** Beginner **TIME:** 4–5 hours

MATERIALS NEEDED:

- Small balloon
- Small torn pieces and strips of old newspaper
- PVA glue mix (50:50, PVA:Water)
- Paintbrushes
- Lightweight card stock
- Embossing tool
- Two 6 x 3-in. (15 x 7.5-cm) and one 3 x 3-in. (7.5 x 7.5-cm) scrunched-up pieces of newspaper, some strips torn from the blank edges
- Scissors
- Double-sided tape
- Pencil
- Yellow, golden brown, cream, red, white, and black acrylic paint
- Elastic cord and tapestry needle
- Tan and brown marabou feathers
- PVA glue
- Craft knife, cutting mat, and ruler

1 Blow up a small balloon and glue small pieces of torn newspaper over one side, top to bottom, with the PVA mix applied with a brush. Paste on an additional three layers of newspaper. Let dry for at least 2 hours; then deflate the balloon and gently peel it away from the inside of the papier-mâché mask.

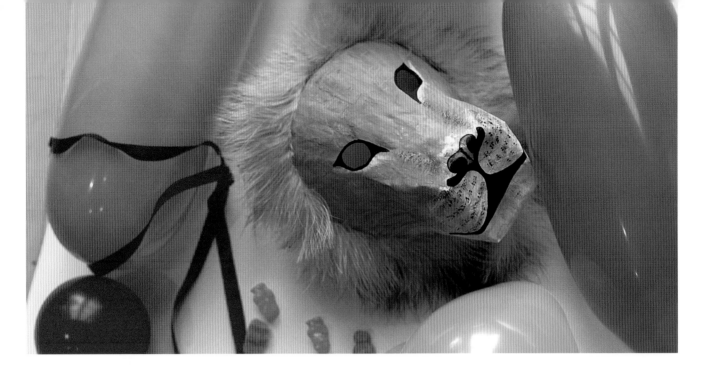

2 Copy the templates for the muzzle on page 169 onto lightweight card and cut out. Score along the fold lines with the embossing tool and make up the muzzle using double-sided tape to attach the nose to the base. Attach to the papier-mâché mask.

3 Fix the 3-in. (7.5-cm) square of scrunched-up newspaper on top of the muzzle for the nose, and the other two pieces on either side. Use the PVA mix to add more strips to create a smooth join with the base, using whiter or blank strips for the top layer.

4 When the newspaper strips are dry, draw two eyes at the top of the muzzle and carefully cut out the holes using a craft knife.

5 Cover the mask in yellow paint. Blend in some golden brown around the top half and cream around the bottom half and on the end of the muzzle. Paint the eyes, nose, and mouth black, applying a little pink to the nose. Stipple black on the muzzle.

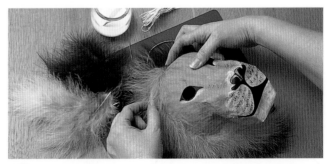

6 Use a needle to make a hole on each side of the mask level with the eyes and thread through a piece of elastic cord, knotting the ends to fasten. To make the mane, fix the brown feathers behind the tan ones around the edge of the mask with PVA glue.

Wrapping and Gifts

Within this chapter you will discover the joy of creating your own packaging for that special handmade gift. There is such a wealth of glorious papers and cards available to the crafter that it is easy to make beautiful baskets and boxes that will suit any occasion. For that truly unique present, why not try your hand at making your own silk paper (see page 112) or decorative handmade stationery, or even jewelry. Using simple techniques, such as quilting, layering, piercing, and collage, you can create a present to delight family and friends, together with gift packaging of all shapes and sizes.

Easter baskets

Make your children's Easter-egg hunt extraspecial this year by giving them their own handmade baskets made from a variety of vellums and decorative papers layered onto card and embellished with ribbons and tacks or snaps. You could also use the pretty baskets for a gift of toiletries, flowering plants, or confectionery.

TECHNIQUES: Stamping, layering, and eyeletting **LEVEL:** Beginner **TIME:** 4–5 hours

MATERIALS NEEDED:

- Pale blue, pale green, and yellow card
- Blue decorative paper
- Vellum
- Pink chalk ink pad
- Floral border stamp
- Baby wipes (alcohol-free)
- $\frac{1}{4}$-in. (6-mm) lilac and peach satin ribbon
- Embossing tool

- Small yellow flower tacks
- $\frac{1}{16}$-in. (1.5-mm)-wide eyeletting punch, hammer, and mat
- Double-sided tape
- PVA glue
- Decorative-edged scissors
- Scissors
- Dry adhesive
- Craft knife, cutting mat, and ruler

1 Enlarge the template on page 165, and use to cut and score the basic basket shape from pale blue card. For the handle, cut a strip of pale blue card $\frac{3}{4}$ x 12 in. (1.5 x 30 cm) and a strip of pale green card $\frac{3}{4}$ x 12$\frac{1}{4}$ in. (2 x 30.5 cm).

2 Use the same template to cut four pieces each of decorative blue paper, vellum, yellow card, and pale green card.

3 Using the pink chalk ink pad, ink the floral border stamp, fading out toward the bottom edge, and stamp it onto the pieces of yellow card (see pages 78–79 for general stamping instructions). Clean the stamp with baby wipes.

4 Trim the top and bottom edges of the yellow card with the decorative-edged scissors.

5 Starting with the blue decorative paper, followed by the yellow card, vellum, and lastly the pale green card, layer up the pieces on each side using dry adhesive.

6 Using double-sided tape, trim the top edge of the green card with the peach ribbon. Apply a smear of PVA glue to each end of the ribbon to stop it from fraying.

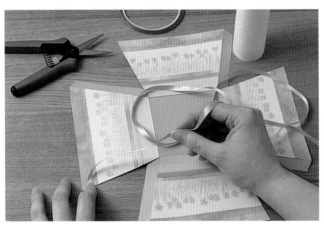

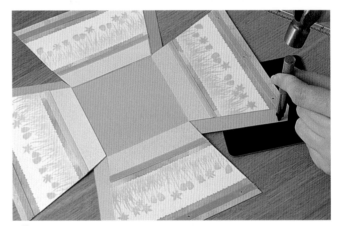

7 Stick lengths of lilac ribbon with double-sided tape to cover the top edges of the vellum, applying PVA glue to each end.

8 Using an eyelet punch, make three small holes in each side—one in the center and one ½ in. (13 mm) from each edge. Make a hole at both ends of the handles. Hold the top corners together. Make a pencil mark where the punched holes fit over the corner flaps.

9 Punch holes in the marked up flaps before sticking double-sided tape down each one to make up the basket. Place yellow flower tacks in each hole, remembering to attach the handles.

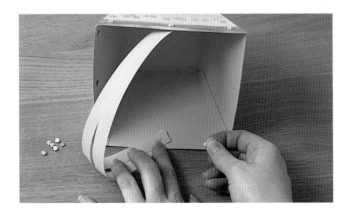

10 **TO MAKE THE SMALL BASKET:** Cut the basket base and handle from pale green card. Cut four strips of decorative vellum 2½ in. (6.5 cm) wide and use a lace border punch to create a decorative edge along one side. Stick a strip on each side of the basket, trim the excess, and make up the basket, fixing the handle with double-sided tape.

11 **TO MAKE THE LARGE BASKET:** Cut the basket base from cream card. Cover each side with a piece of pale yellow card. Layer up with torn-edged yellow paper, daisy-printed vellum, and butterfly-printed trim. Using a craft punch, create daisies out of yellow and pale yellow vellum.

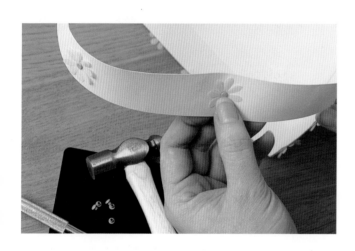

12 Punch five equidistant holes along the top of each edge and three more on the handle. Using an eyeletting tool, fix the daisies in position with an orange snap through each hole, also affixing the handle. Finish making up the basket and fix a 1-in. (2.5-cm) strip of yellow card around the top inner edge. Cut a gift tag and thread with ribbon onto the basket.

CRAFTER'S TIP

When stamping, you don't need to ink the entire stamp. You can choose to ink only part of it, allowing it to fade out, as has been done here. Alternatively, you can mask part of the stamp with low-tack masking tape, ink it as normal, then remove the masking tape before stamping.

Colorwash book cover & bookmark

Trying to find that truly special gift for a loved one is never easy. How about making your own with this heart-themed patchwork bookmark and matching paper-quilted book? When creating colorwash decorative paper, you will find that no two pieces are exactly the same.

TECHNIQUES: Colorwashing, stamping, patchwork, quilting **LEVEL:** Beginner and Intermediate **TIME:** 7–9 hours

MATERIALS NEEDED

For the decorated paper:
- 140 lb. (300 gsm) watercolor paper
- Old board
- Masking tape
- Red, purple, and blue acrylic paints
- Brush, palette, and water
- Water-soluble metallic powders, such as calligraphy powders
- Plastic food wrap
- Wet-strength tissue paper

For the bookmark:
- PVA glue
- Bronze ink pad
- Large heart stamp
- 3-D clear lacquer
- Baby wipes (alcohol-free)
- Clear ink pad
- Cranberry and eggplant embossing powders
- Embossing heat tool
- Eyeletting tools
- Pink heart eyelet
- Thin leather thong
- Assorted beads
- Small heart-shaped gems
- Industrial-strength adhesive
- Craft knife, cutting mat, and ruler

For the book cover:
- 6 x 6-in. (15 x 15-cm) book kit
- White cotton
- 1-in. (2.5-cm)-thick polyester fiber wadding
- Color-coordinated thread
- Large needle and pins
- Copper heart-shaped brads
- Large heart gem
- Color-coordinated fashion yarn
- Cream card
- Double-sided tape
- Sewing machine

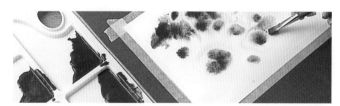

1 TO MAKE THE DECORATIVE PAPER: Tape the watercolor paper to an old board and, using a brush, wet it thoroughly with water.

2 Randomly apply watered-down acrylic paints to the paper; then sprinkle over water-soluble metallic powder, which will dissolve on impact.

3 Cover the paper with a large piece of plastic food wrap, scrunch it up to create the pattern, and leave the paper to dry with the plastic wrap in place. Decorate the tissue paper in the same way.

4 **TO MAKE THE BOOKMARK:** Cut out 14 squares measuring 1⅕ in. (3 cm) from the decorated watercolor paper. Using a bronze ink pad, stamp a large heart on one square. Cover this square with a coat of 3-D lacquer and let it dry.

5 Position the squares onto the back of another piece of decorated paper with the lacquered square at the top, as shown, and stick in place with PVA glue. Cut the bookmark to size, using the corners of the outer squares as a guide.

6 In clear embossing ink, stamp small hearts in the center of the half squares and emboss with cranberry and eggplant embossing powders. Melt the powders with a heat tool. Refer to page 131 for instructions on stamping and embossing.

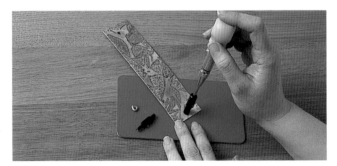

7 Punch a hole at the base of the bookmark, using an eyeletting tool, and fix the pink heart eyelet.

8 Thread assorted beads onto each end of an 8½-in. (22-cm) length of leather thong and tie through the eyelet. At each end of the thong, glue two small hearts back to back, squashing the thong between them.

9 **TO MAKE THE BOOK COVER:** Cut an 8¼-in. (21-cm) square from the wet-strength tissue paper. Cut a piece of cotton and a piece of wadding 6½ x 5¼ in. (16.5 x 13.5 cm). Sandwich the wadding between the cotton and tissue; pin diagonal stitching lines to create a diamond quilt pattern. Stitch together.

10 Using a large needle, make holes just above some of the stitched intersections and fix heart-shaped brads in place.

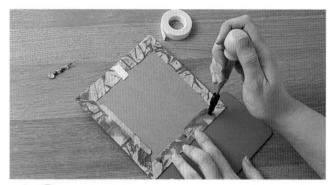

11 Cover the front of the book with a piece of cream card. Stick on the quilted paper, as shown, wrapping the excess paper around the edges and fixing on the reverse.

12 Thread some beads on one end of a piece of the thong and flatten the other end. Using a piece of double-sided tape, stick this toward the outer edge. Repunch the holes down the edge of the cover.

13 Cut another piece of cream card slightly smaller than the cover and stick to the inside to neaten. Repunch the holes again.

14 Repeat Steps 11 to 13 with a plain piece of decorated tissue for the back cover. Finish the book by sticking a large heart gem in the central diamond, and binding loosely with fashion yarn.

Paper bead jewelry

With so many gorgeous papers available today there is no end to the attractive beads you can create that can then be made up into unusual jewelry. To take it a step further, you could make your own paper as well—then your necklace and earrings will be truly unique!

TECHNIQUE: Paper beadmaking **LEVEL:** Beginner **TIME:** 3–4 hours

MATERIALS NEEDED

For decorated paper:
- Indian cotton rag paper
- Powdered pigments
- Brush
- White and gold spray webbing
- Pearly powders
- Hair spray

For the paper bead jewelry:
- Decorative papers
- PVA glue
- Industrial-strength instant adhesive
- Toothpick
- Decorative-edged scissors
- Tweezers
- 16 small clear round gems
- 4-in. (10-cm) piece of wire and jewelry jump ring
- 2 large teardrop clear gems
- Silver wire beads
- Seed beads
- Memory wire necklace
- Earring findings
- Pliers
- Wire cutters
- Craft knife, cutting mat, and ruler

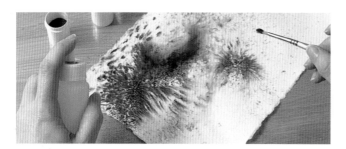

1 TO MAKE THE DECORATED PAPER FOR THE DARK BEADS: Wet a piece of Indian cotton rag paper with water and apply pigment powders by dropping or tapping the powder from a brush. Leave to dry.

The silver wire beads and gems add a touch of luxury.

2 When the paper and pigment are dry, spray an even layer of white webbing across the paper. Make sure that you are working in a well-ventilated room. Leave to dry.

3 **TO MAKE THE DECORATED PAPER FOR THE LIGHT BEADS:** In a well-ventilated room, spray white and gold webbing onto a piece of Indian cotton rag paper. Leave for a few minutes to dry.

4 Using your fingertips, gently rub a mixture of pearly powders into the paper. Fix the powders with a fine layer of hair spray.

5 **TO MAKE THE PAPER BEAD JEWELRY:** Using the decorative paper made in Steps 1 to 4, for each large bead, cut one long tapering strip measuring ⅜ x 8 in. (1 x 20 cm), and for each small bead, ⅜ x 4 in. (1 x 10 cm).

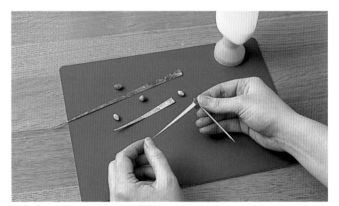

6 Starting with the wider end, tightly roll each strip of decorated paper around a toothpick (or cockail stick). Add a spot of PVA glue to secure the ends. Make the bugle bead in the same way but with a piece ⅜ x 8 in. (1 x 20 cm) long with 3 in. (7.5 cm) removed from the tapered end.

7 For bell-shaped beads, as used in the earrings (see right and page 105), slide the tapered point of a bugle bead to one side.

CRAFTER'S TIP

Make matching earrings (see page 105) by threading beads onto a wire post and sticking a small gem at the base. Use pliers to create a loop at the top and cut the excess with wire cutters. Attach these to wire earring findings.

8 For the bugle bead, use tweezers to carefully add four tiny gems around each bead, using industrial-strength instant adhesive.

9 To create the center pendant, take two small pieces of decorative paper and place them right sides together. Cut a teardrop shape using decorative-edged scissors. Glue the wrong sides together with PVA glue, sandwiching the ends of a small, folded length of wire in between.

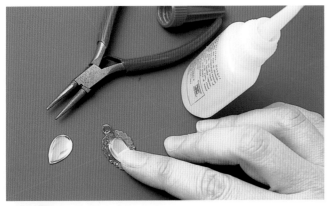

10 Glue a teardrop gem on each side of the pendant. Use jewelry pliers to open up a jump ring and thread it through the wire loop before closing it.

11 Thread your beads onto a memory wire necklace, starting with the pendant and then adding paper beads interspersed with wire beads in a matching sequence on each side. Secure by sticking a small seed bead on each end of the wire.

Pillow box

This pretty pillow box is a gift in itself, but it can be used to encase any small present, such as jewelry, perfume, a silk scarf, or even a special handkerchief or two. Here, handmade batik paper (see the Crafter's Tip) has been used for a stunning effect, but any heavyweight paper or lightweight card can be used instead.

TECHNIQUES: Paper punching and layering **LEVEL:** Beginner **TIME:** 2–3 hours

MATERIALS NEEDED:

- Handmade batik paper
- Embossed paper
- Vellum
- Sticky-back holographic paper
- Embossing tool
- Dry stick glue
- Eyelets and eyeletting tools
- 12-in. (30-cm) ribbon, ³⁄₈ in. (1 cm) wide
- Letter die-cut templates
- Die-cut machine
- Scissors
- Craft knife, cutting mat, and ruler

CRAFTER'S TIP

To create handmade batik paper, first make some heavyweight paper (see pages 16 to 18). Draw your design on the paper using a paintbrush and melted wax; then wet and dye the paper. When the paper is dry, cover with brown paper and iron over it; then apply metallic paint.

1 Using the template on page 170, cut out the batik paper and embossed paper following the solid line, and the vellum using the outer, dashed line. Score the fold lines with an embossing tool.

2 Lay the batik paper facedown and stick the vellum over it, as shown. Then stick the embossed paper faceup over the layers.

3 Punch four evenly spaced holes on the face of the pillow box $\frac{3}{16}$ in. (5 mm) in from the curved fold lines at either side.

4 Fix color-coordinated eyelets in each hole using the eyelet setter.

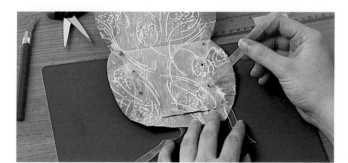

5 For the ribbon tie, using the template as a guide, make two small cuts at either end and thread through short lengths of ribbon, securing them with knots. Thread a ribbon through the eyelets at each end, tying knots in the corners. Trim the excess.

6 Use the die cuts to punch out the initials of the recipient of the gift in the holographic paper. Make up the box. Glue the initials to a small square of batik paper; then stick the batik to the front of the pillow box.

Marbled gift wrap

Marbling is fun to do and is a great way to create some wonderfully patterned paper for use in all sorts of projects. Here it has been used as gift wrap, but it can also be used as a background for card making. You can use this technique on fabric, as well as paper.

TECHNIQUE: Marbling LEVEL: Beginner TIME: 4–5 hours

MATERIALS NEEDED:
- Water bath (a brand-new litter tray is ideal), jug, and teaspoon
- Selection of water-based marbling inks in various colors
- Marbling medium
- Toothpick, embossing tool, or marbling comb
- Paper

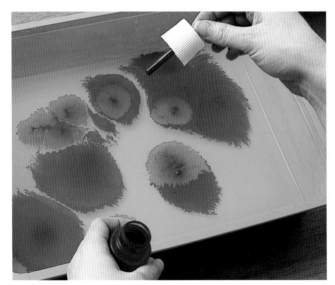

1 Fill the bath with water and carefully stir in the marbling medium following the manufacturer's instructions. Leave to thicken. Randomly drop on the inks.

2 Use a toothpick, embossing tool, or marbling comb to drag out the colors, creating your pattern. If any air bubbles appear, pop them with a dry finger.

3 Taking care not to trap air beneath the paper, lower the sheet onto the surface and leave for 10 to 15 seconds.

4 Starting at one corner, slowly peel the paper off the medium.

5 Hold the paper briefly under gently running water to remove the excess medium; then place on one side to dry. Each sheet will be unique and each successive sheet will get paler unless more ink is added.

Silk paper gift bag

This project shows you how to make a very unusual gift bag using your own handmade silk paper, perfect for a present such as the paper bead jewelry featured on page 104. Embellished with a lace trim, it is sure to impress the person who receives it.

TECHNIQUE: Silk papermaking **LEVEL:** Beginner **TIME:** 2–3 hours

MATERIALS NEEDED:

- Silk papermaking paste
- Plastic sheeting or bin liner
- Piece of net
- Silk fibers
- Sponge
- Water spray
- Eyeletting punch
- Embossing tool
- Color-coordinated or plain card
- Double-sided tape
- Decorative wire or ribbon
- Lace
- PVA glue and paintbrush
- Craft knife, cutting mat, and ruler

1 Make up the paste as per the manufacturer's instructions and protect your work surface with plastic. Lay down a piece of net twice the size of your desired paper and, in a crisscrossing fashion, lay the teased-out silk fibers on one half.

2 Fold the net over on top of the fibers and use a water spray to dampen. Using a sponge, apply the paste through the net. Work methodically from left to right until the whole piece is covered, making sure the paste has gone right through. Remove the excess paste and let dry for 30 minutes.

3 Peel the net away from the silk paper. Use PVA glue to stick this to a color-coordinated piece of card and let dry.

4 Use the bag template on page 170 to cut your silk card. Punch four holes at the top for attaching the handles.

5 Score the fold lines with the embossing tool. Make up the bag using double-sided tape to fix the flap, then the base.

6 Use ribbon or decorative wire for the handles. To finish, edge the bag with lace, gluing it to the top of the bag.

CRAFTER'S TIP

If you use fewer fibers, the paper will be very fine and will need to be stuck to card. If you use more fibers and more paste, the paper will be strong enough on its own.

Wedding stationery

Make your invitations stand out from the crowd with your own handmade-paper wedding stationery. If you are having a dress made, ask for a remnant of material to cut up into tiny squares and embed them in the paper. As an alternative to the dried rosebuds used here, press small flowers that you intend to have in your bouquet and sandwich them between the mesh.

TECHNIQUE: Papermaking with inclusions **LEVEL:** Intermediate **TIME:** 5–6 hours (plus drying time for paper)

MATERIALS NEEDED:

- Fine white mesh (Angel-hair fiber)
- Plastic pocket
- Dried rosebuds
- Papermaking tools (see page 16)
- Cotton linter
- Silk material squares and threads
- Rose-colored card
- Silk thread
- Beads and charms
- Silver gilding wax
- Tissue

- Die-cut machine
- Letter and numerical die-cut templates
- Insert papers printed with wedding details, 5⅞ x 7⅞ in. (15 x 20 cm)
- Dry adhesive
- PVA glue
- Lickable envelope glue
- Scissors
- Craft knife, cutting mat, and ruler

1 For every invitation or piece of stationery that you plan to make, cut two 2-in. (5-cm) squares of mesh. Lay one square on a plastic pocket. Apply a touch of PVA glue to the back of a dried rosebud and position it in the center of the mesh square.

2 Apply a thin line of PVA glue all around the edge of the square and position the other mesh square over the top, sandwiching the rosebud in between. Leave to dry.

3 Use a pencil to mark the mesh edges on the 5 x 7-in. (13 x 18-cm) papermaking frame. (This will help you get the mesh in exactly the same position every time.) Use the template on page 171 as a guide to mask off a 1½-in. (4-cm) square with masking tape.

4 Put enough cotton linter pulp into the papermaking vat to create a thin piece of paper. Insert the frame and mesh and raise them to the surface of the water, allowing them to float with the loaded layer of pulp.

5 Drop on the silk threads and silk squares, gently pressing them into the pulp before lifting the frame out and letting the water drain off.

6 Making sure to line up one corner of the mesh with the drying sheet, transfer the pulp and press out the excess water.

7 Remove any stray pieces of pulp from the aperture and place the paper on one side. Load the mesh with more pulp, this time without any inclusions.

8 Lay the loaded mesh on the towel and position a rosebud fiber square faceup over the aperture. Lining up the same corner, lay the preloaded drying sheet on top, trapping the edges of the fiber square between the two sheets. Press out the excess water, remove the mesh, and let dry overnight.

9 Use the die-cut machine to punch out the couple's initials from the rose-colored card. Before removing them from the card, lightly rub some silver gilding wax over the top with a tissue.

10 Using dry adhesive, position the initials beneath the rosebud aperture, as shown. With a tissue carefully apply more gilding wax to the edges of the paper before folding the invitation in half.

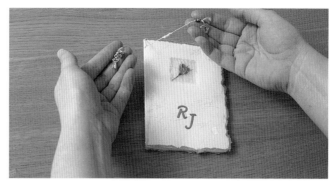

11 Fold the printed insert paper in half with the text on the inside. Place this inside the invitation and, to hold the card and insert together, tie a length of silk threaded with beads and charms around the fold.

12 Use the templates on page 171 to mask the small and large papermaking meshes for the "save the date" card and envelope. Then follow Steps 4 to 7 to make the paper.

13 Follow Steps 8 to 9 to punch, gild, and attach the date and initials for the "save the date" card. Gild the edges and fold the stationery, sticking the envelope as shown.

14 Use a length of silk thread with beads and charms to hold the printed insert in position for the "save the date" card, as in Step 11.

15 Make two small cuts in the flap of the envelope and thread through a small length of decorated silk thread, tying the ends together to secure. Apply some lickable glue to the edge of the flap.

Decorative stationery

Impress your friends by giving them their own handmade personalized stationery. You can tailor it to their tastes by making it in their favorite color, and instead of using an initial, you can choose to use a stamp that will reflect their individual passion or hobby; for example, gardening, pets, or sports.

TECHNIQUE: Papermaking with embossing **LEVEL:** Intermediate **TIME:** 3–4 hours (plus drying time for paper)

MATERIALS NEEDED:
- Papermaking equipment (see page 16)
- Cotton linter
- Blue tissue paper
- Tracing paper
- Stamp
- Decorating chalks
- Hair spray
- Water spray
- Embossing tool
- Single-needle tool
- Thread
- Enameled charms
- Double-sided tape
- Craft knife, cutting mat, and ruler

1 Make some 5 x 7 in. (13 x 18 cm) paper using cotton linter, tracing paper, and blue tissue (see pages 16 to18). When dry, turn the paper faceup and lay it on the drying sheet. Spray with water and press the stamp firmly in position, then carefully remove.

2 When the paper is dry, remove it from the drying sheet and gently rub some blue decorating chalk over the image to bring out the design. Spray lightly with hair spray to fix the chalk. Make envelopes to match using the template on page 171.

3 For the folder, make two 8½ x 11-in. (21 x 30-cm) sheets and, when dry, cut 3⅜ in. (8.5 cm) from the end of one sheet. Fold over ⅝ in. (1.5 cm) on the cut edge and the two adjacent sides. Fix a loop of thread slightly wider than the narrow side of the charm in the center, 2¾ in. (7 cm) from the unfolded side.

4 Take the second sheet and fold over ⅝ in. (1.5 cm) on the two longer sides and a short side. Add a 2¾-in. (7-cm)-long charm tie to the center of the unfolded side ⅜ in. (1 cm) from the edge. Score a line approximately 2 in. (5 cm) from the tie end.

5 Place the second sheet on the work surface with the folded edges facing up. Stick double-sided tape down the folds and attach a 9⅝ x 6¹¹⁄₁₆-in. (25 x 17-cm) piece of blue tissue.

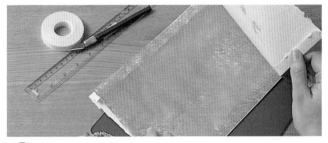

6 Stick double-sided tape along the flaps of the other piece of paper and stick in position, lining up the bottom edges to create the folder.

Vintage keepsake box

Vintage papers together with miniature postcards, label stickers, and old postage stamps have been used to decorate this keepsake box. Trimmed with ribbon and lace, it is the perfect place to store those treasured items, such as love letters or a baby's first bootees.

TECHNIQUE: Collage **LEVEL:** Intermediate **TIME:** 6–7 hours

MATERIALS NEEDED:

- Papier-mâché box
- PVA glue and brush
- Decorative papers and fibers
- Embellishments: stickers, transfers, mini postcards, and old postage stamps
- Gold lock or clasp
- Pliers
- Lace trim and thin ribbon
- Woven cotton tape
- Scissors
- Craft knife, cutting mat, and ruler

1 Using PVA glue and a brush, apply various pieces of decorative paper to completely cover the outside of the box, overlapping them as you build up the collage. Vary the size of the pieces.

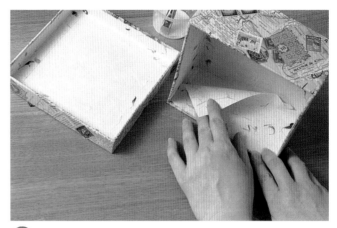

2 Glue assorted embellishments to the box, such as tag stickers threaded with fibers, old stamps, mini postcards, and rub-ons or transfers.

3 Measure the inner side of the box and cut four strips of paper ⅜ in. (1 cm) taller. Stick these inside. Repeat for the lid.

4 Measure the inside base of the box and cut a square of paper slightly smaller. Stick this on the bottom. Repeat for the lid.

5 Thread ribbon through the top of the length of lace and attach this around the top edge of the lid with PVA glue.

CRAFTER'S TIP

You will find it easier to thread the ribbon through the top of the lace if you use a small safety pin. Attach the safety pin to the end of the ribbon and use this like a bobbin to weave evenly in and out of the lace.

The small gold clasp attached to the cotton tape could be replaced with a lock-and-key mechanism for more privacy.

6 Use pliers to attach part of the gold clasp to one end of the cotton tape. Attach this end to the center of one side of the box with PVA glue. Wrap the tape around the box, sticking it to the center of the opposite side. Trim the excess tape before attaching the other half of the clasp.

New-baby scrapbook

A small scrapbook to capture the first few months of a baby's life would be a perfect gift for new grandparents. Having decorated the cover as below, either complete the book, as shown right, or start by decorating the first couple of pages and leave the rest to complete as time goes on.

TECHNIQUE: Scrapbooking **LEVEL:** Beginner **TIME:** 3–4 hours

MATERIALS NEEDED:

- Pink paper
- Lace border punch
- Silver initial brads
- Baby carriage glue motif
- Ultrafine pink glitter
- Acid-free double-sided tape
- Ready-made leaf-green mini scrapbook cover
- Acid-free adhesive
- Bow motif
- Ready-made mini insert pages
- Craft knife, cutting mat, and ruler

1 Cut out a piece of pink paper 4¾ x 4½ in. (12 x 11.5 cm). Using a lace border punch, create a decorative edge along the two shorter sides.

2 Make small cuts about 1 in. (2.5 cm) from the top to enable you to fix the silver initial brads in place.

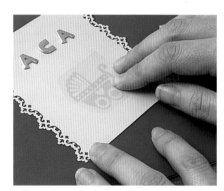

3 Take the baby carriage glue motif and position this under the initials on the pink paper.

4 Peel away the protective backing on the baby carriage motif. Sprinkle ultrafine glitter over the top and tip off the excess. Use a soft brush to remove any stubborn glitter. Use double-sided tape to fix the paper centrally at the top of the book cover.

5 Cut out the bow motif and fix with acid-free adhesive beneath the pink paper. Thread the ribbon tie through the slots provided and insert your chosen book pages.

6 Don't forget to decorate the fly leaf. You could punch a stork die-cut from coordinating pearlescent paper and attach it to the center of the vellum fly leaf.

Oriental gift box

How about this for an unusual gift box? These pyramid-shaped boxes could be used to wrap a piece of jewelry for a special birthday present or to enclose a few handmade chocolates as a dinner-party favor. If you wish, you could attach a matching gift card to the red cotton ties.

MATERIALS NEEDED:

- Red card
- Embossing tool
- White washi paper
- Dry glue stick
- Silver ink pad
- Fan stamp
- Baby wipes (alcohol-free)
- Scissors
- Small clear gems
- PVA glue
- Eyeletting punch
- Red cotton thread and needle
- Decorative beads
- Craft knife, cutting mat, and ruler

1 Cut out the red base card using the template supplied on page 172. Using the embossing tool, score where indicated by dotted lines.

2 Use the same template to cut the four pieces of washi paper and fix these in position on the red base card with a dry glue stick.

3 Ink the stamp with silver ink and stamp onto another piece of red card. Repeat three times; then clean the stamp with a baby wipe. (This stamp featured several fans, so only the central part was inked.)

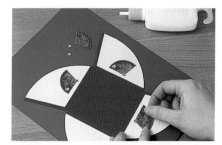

4 Using scissors, cut out the four fans and stick them onto the washi. Stick a small clear gem onto each fan with a dab of PVA glue.

5 Use an eyeletting punch to create evenly spaced holes around the base of the box.

6 Cut four lengths of red cotton thread to use as the ties. Thread some decorative beads on the end of each. Make a hole at the apex of each side with a needle, thread the ties on, and knot the thread. Secure the knot with a dab of PVA glue.

Scented parchment sachets

If you've never tried parchment craft before but fancy a challenge, then try this project as a way to learn some of the techniques. You have the choice of whether to paint a design in the center, as in the drawer sachet, or rubber-stamp one for the closet sachet (right). Scented sachets are an ideal present for that female relative or friend "who has everything."

TECHNIQUE: Parchment craft **LEVEL:** Advanced **TIME:** 5–6 hours

MATERIALS NEEDED:

- Large sheet of vellum
- Embossing tool
- Crimson and blue oil pastels
- Parchment blending oil and tissue
- Low-tack masking tape
- Felt pad
- Semicircle tool
- 5-needle tool
- Star tool
- Square tool
- Mapping pen
- White ink
- Small paintbrush
- Crimson, blue, and green inks
- Palette
- Thin double-sided tape
- Thin lavender ribbon
- Tweezers
- Lavender potpourri
- PVA glue
- Craft knife, cutting mat, and ruler
- Floral rubber stamp
- Violet pigment ink pad
- Silver pearl embossing powder
- Heat-embossing tool
- Small brush
- Baby wipes

1 **TO MAKE THE DRAWER SACHET:** Enlarge the template on page 172 and trace onto the sheet of vellum. Cut out the sachet template and score along the guides using an embossing tool.

2 On the wrong side of the vellum, lightly color the edges of the central square and the leading edges of each flap with the oil pastels. Gently blend the colors together with a tissue soaked in a little oil.

3 Turn the vellum over, temporarily fix it on the template with some low-tack masking tape, and place it on the felt pad. Use the semicircle tool, 5-needle tool, and star tool to prick out the corner designs.

4 Use the square tool to create the little squares, being careful to reach the same depth and therefore creating the same-size hole for each one except the second one in from each corner, which should be larger.

5 Remove the vellum from the felt pad. Trace the lavender design in the center of the sachet with the mapping pen and white ink. Let it dry for a couple of minutes before painting the stems of the lavender with the green ink and the lavender buds and bow with a mix of crimson, blue, and white ink.

6 Remove the vellum from the template and, using thin double-sided tape, stick strips of ribbon from each corner of the sachet to the curl of each flap. Stick more double-sided tape on top of the ribbon. Close three sides of the sachet and with tweezers remove the backing from the tape to fix two flaps in position.

7 Fill the sachet with lavender potpourri before tucking the last flap into position and removing the remaining two backing strips to secure the flap in place with the potpourri inside.

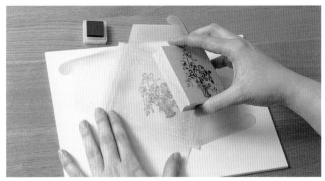

8 **TO MAKE THE CLOSET SACHET:** Instead of tracing the central design, ink the floral stamp with the violet pigment ink and stamp this in the center of the vellum.

CRAFTER'S TIP

When stamping on vellum, you must use either a pigment ink pad and then emboss it, or a permanent ink pad, which will dry on nonporous surfaces. Dye-based ink pads will dry, but if they get damp at any time, the ink will reactivate and smudge. A pigment ink pad will never dry and so must be embossed to seal the ink.

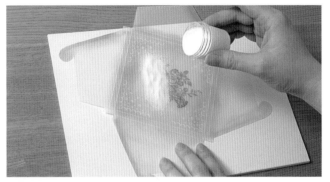

9 Shake silver pearl embossing powder over the inked floral image.

10 Tip off the excess powder and return this to the pot. Use a brush to remove any loose bits of unwanted powder.

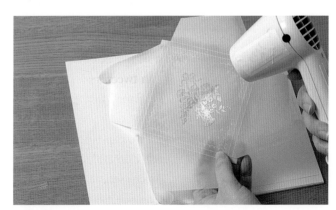

11 Use a heat-embossing tool to melt the powder on the image. Don't forget to clean your stamp with a baby wipe or stamp cleaner.

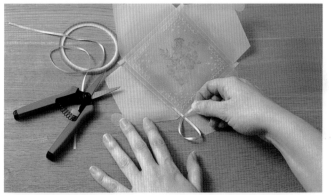

12 To make a hanging loop, cut the small flap from the top corner of the sachet. Fix the ends of a small loop of ribbon to each top edge. Follow Steps 6 to 7 to fill and close the sachet before adding a touch of PVA glue to seal the ribbon corner.

Secret keepsake box

Altered art is the technique used to change an object's use and at the same time create a work of art. This project will show you how to create a secret compartment within an old book (see top picture page 134) and how to start decorating the pages. It's up to you how much further you take it—see the example opposite.

TECHNIQUE: Altered art **LEVEL:** Advanced **TIME:** 4–5 hours

MATERIALS NEEDED:

- Old hardback book
- Acid-free adhesive
- Acid-free narrow double-sided tape
- Matte medium
- Iridescent violet, misty lavender, and duo red-blue pearl powders
- Round and flat brushes
- Plastic pocket
- Draftboard clips
- Decorative lilac paper
- Handmade paper with inclusions
- White Japanese lace paper
- Waxed thread
- Decorative brad
- Cigarette lighter
- Eyeletting punch
- Scissors
- Craft knife, cutting mat, and ruler

1 Using a dab of acid-free adhesive, sandwich one end of the waxed thread between two pages toward the back of the book so that it sticks out 4–5 in. (10–12.5 cm). With a flat brush, spread acid-free adhesive along the three edges of a thick block of pages to stick them together. Hold them in position with draftboard clips and let dry for approximately 30 minutes.

2 Using a sharp craft knife, cut out a section in the middle of the stuck block, removing clumps of pages as you go. You can choose whether you cut all the way through to the back page or only partway through—it depends how deep you want the compartment to be.

3 Use more adhesive to stick the block to the back cover and to brush along the edges of the recess. Affix the clips in position, holding the block together as in Step 1; then let dry.

As an extra, decorate the page with ink and colored vellums.

4 Using acid-free adhesive or double-sided tape, line the compartment with a piece of decorative lilac paper. Carefully cut away the excess with a knife or scissors.

5 On the first loose page adjacent to the front of the block, mark the edges of the recess with pencil. Cut slits diagonally from corner to corner both ways. Use a wet brush to draw a wavy waterline $\frac{3}{16}-\frac{3}{8}$ in. (5 mm–1 cm) from the edge of the cut marks. Carefully singe the edges of the flaps using the cigarette lighter. The waterline should stop the page from burning further, but be ready to apply more water if necessary. Stick this page to the top of the compartment block with acid-free adhesive.

6 Mix some matte medium with the pearl colors and apply to the front of the page with a brush. While still wet, fold back the flaps so that they stick to the medium and cover the top edge of the compartment. Apply more medium on top and let dry for approximately 20 minutes.

7 Take the next two loose pages and cut a hole in the center of them. Using the technique described in Step 5, singe the edges of the holes. Halfway down the first of these two pages, measure approximately $\frac{3}{8}$ in. (1 cm) in from the outside edge and fix a decorative brad. When you have finished decorating the book, you will be able to wind the waxed thread around this to keep the compartment hidden.

8 Sandwich a piece of lace paper between these two pages and, protecting the rest of the book with a plastic pocket, stick them together with acid-free adhesive. Let dry.

9 Remove the next ten loose pages from the book. Using a knife and ruler, cut a piece of handmade paper and a piece of lace paper the same width as a page but two thirds the height.

10 Cut the handmade paper almost in half lengthwise, to ½ in. (13 mm) above the bottom edge. Measure 1½ in. (4 cm) down the center line on each piece. Draw a line from this point to the top-outer edge with a wet brush and ruler, and gently tear apart, leaving soft edges.

11 Using narrow double-sided tape along the bottom and down the sides, stick the lace paper to the back of the next loose page opposite the block. Punch small holes at ½-in. (12-mm) intervals down the center edges of the handmade paper.

12 Lace the two edges of handmade paper together with waxed thread, and with more double-sided tape along the bottom and side edges, stick this on top of the lace paper. If necessary, stick more loose pages together to give this extra support.

Creative Cards

Cardmaking is always extremely popular with crafters, probably because we all need greetings cards to send to friends and family to celebrate birthdays, anniversaries, and other special occasions. Cards are also an excellent way to dabble in a new craft, to see if you enjoy it before investing in a lot of equipment. In this chapter you will see how easy it is to incorporate decoupage, patchwork, paper folding, origami, and parchment craft within your card designs. All of these techniques can be expanded upon for use in other projects should you decide you would like to take them further.

Decoupage birthday cards

Inspiration should never fail you when using decoupage. With so many stamps, die cuts, and decoupage papers, you'll have many choices when it comes to the theme for your card. The length of time needed will depend on how complicated your chosen design is.

TECHNIQUE: Decoupage and 3-D decoupage **LEVEL:** Beginner **TIME:** 2–3 hours

MATERIALS NEEDED

For the panda card:
- Panda stamp
- Permanent black ink pad
- Sticky foam pads
- Die-cut machine and tag templates
- Green-leaf patterned paper
- Cream and white paper
- 6⁷⁄₈-in. (17.5-cm) piece of gold crepe paper
- 2⁵⁄₁₆ x 6⁷⁄₈-in. (6 x 17.5-cm) strip of brown suede-effect paper
- Thin cream ribbon
- 5 x 7 in. (12.5 x 17.5 cm) cream blank card
- Scissors
- Double-sided tape

For the fairy card:
- Faerie decoupage paper
- Purple glitter star paper
- 5 x 7 in. (12.5 x 17.5 cm) white oval aperture card
- Sticky foam pads
- Ultrafine glitter
- PVA glue
- Purple foil and foil glue pen
- Scissors
- Double-sided tape
- 3-D silver glitter paint
- Craft knife, cutting mat, and ruler

1 **TO MAKE THE PANDA CARD:** Using the black ink pad, stamp the panda image nine times onto pieces of white paper. Clean the stamp with stamp cleaner.

2 Cut out: three complete designs; the head, hands, bamboo, and feet from another three; just the hands and feet of the remaining three pandas.

3 Using the complete design as a base, stick the layers on top using double-sided sticky foam pads.

4 Use a die-cut machine to punch three small scalloped tags from the green leaf paper and three large scalloped tags from the cream paper. Thread a small piece of ribbon through each green tag.

5 Stick the green tags on top of the larger cream ones. Then stick a panda on each green tag.

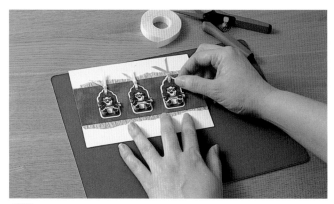

6 Place the brown suede-effect paper over the gold crepe paper to use as a guide, and tear the top and bottom edges to give a width of 3 in. (7.5 cm). Stick the crepe paper across the center of the card.

7 Use double-sided tape to layer the strip of brown suede-effect paper on top of the gold crepe paper and then position the panda tags at equidistant intervals along it.

8 **TO MAKE THE FAIRY CARD:** Cut out the fairy design and layer the pieces using double-sided sticky foam pads.

9 Using double-sided tape, stick the purple decorative paper behind the oval aperture on the inside of the card.

10 Use more double-sided tape to stick the fairy in position inside the aperture on the purple backing paper.

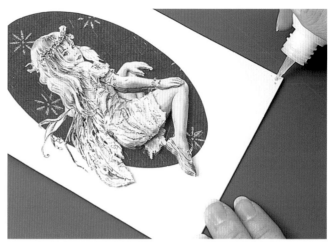

11 Apply three small dots of silver glitter 3-D paint to each corner of the card.

12 Use a glue pen to apply small dashes around the edge of the exposed aperture.

13 Let the glue dry for several minutes before applying the purple foil by gently rubbing over the dashes of glue.

14 Apply PVA glue to small areas of the fairy design and sprinkle ultrafine glitter over the top. Let it dry before brushing off the excess glitter.

CRAFTER'S TIP

You don't have to use decoupage papers to create 3-D decoupage cards. You can make your own by rubber-stamping an image several times or use preprinted items such as gift tags.

Celebration card

Create a truly unique congratulations card to celebrate a wedding, engagement, or anniversary by following these simple step-by-step instructions. By using a different motif with the patchwork background, you could make a card for a new baby, coming of age, or graduation.

TECHNIQUE: Patchwork **LEVEL:** Intermediate **TIME:** 1–2 hours

MATERIALS NEEDED:

- Cream card and paper
- Purple, green, and blue papers
- Double-sided tape
- 2¼ x 5¼-in. (6 x 13-cm) cream embossed paper
- Pearl and clear three-dimensional paint
- 0.3 mm ultrafine metal nib
- Acetate
- Ultrafine iridescent glitter
- Glitter paper
- PVA and lickable glue
- Cutting mat, ruler, scissors, and craft knife

1 Using the craft knife and ruler, cut a piece of cream card measuring 9 x 7½ in. (23 x 19 cm). Using the back of the craft knife, score a fold line halfway along the long edge and fold to make a card 4½ x 7½ in. (11.5 x 19 cm).

2 Cut 24 x ¾-in. (2-cm) squares of purple, green, and blue paper. Stick eight squares on double-sided tape. Repeat with another eight squares, then two strips of four. Position the strips around the piece of embossed paper.

3 Peel off the remaining backing strip on the double-sided tape and fix in position on the cream card.

4 Using the pearl three-dimensional paint with the metal nib, draw small stitch marks across all the paper edges. Leave to dry.

5 Copy the template of the champagne flute (see page 173) and, using scissors, cut two flutes from the sheet of acetate.

6 Smear a little clear three-dimensional paint across the top rim of the acetate flutes and sprinkle some ultrafine glitter over the top. Tip off the excess and return it to the pot. Leave to dry.

7 Stick the flutes onto the top of the card with a small dab of clear three-dimensional paint.

8 Use the clear three-dimensional paint to make little dots to resemble bubbles around the top of the flutes; then sprinkle some ultrafine glitter over the top. Tip off the excess glitter, returning it to the pot.

9 Enlarge the smaller, inset template (see page 173) and use to cut a small envelope out of the glitter paper.

10 Following the template, use the back of the craft knife and a ruler to score the fold lines on the small glitter envelope.

11 Fold and make up the envelope carefully, using a small amount of PVA glue on the edges of the flaps.

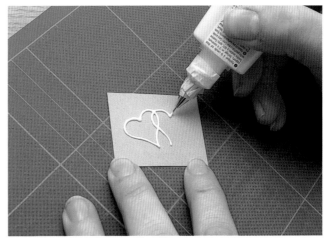

12 Cut out a piece of green paper, measuring 1½ x 2 in. (4 x 5 cm). Draw two interlocking hearts onto this paper with the pearl three-dimensional paint and let dry.

13 Use a craft knife to scrape a little glitter from the front of the envelope to allow you to stick this facedown along with the green paper at the bottom of the card, as shown.

14 Enlarge and copy the large envelope template on page 173 and make it up in cream paper to match the card. Apply a strip of lickable glue around the top flap. Leave to dry.

CRAFTER'S TIP

If you have an embossing tool in your craft kit, you can use this instead of the back of a craft knife to score the fold lines in the paper and card.

Scrapbook card

This is the perfect card for those friends and family you haven't seen for some time. Mat a recent photo of your child or the whole family on the decorative paper before inserting it into the pouch. You can personalize the front of the card with your own message before sending it.

TECHNIQUE: Scrapbooking **LEVEL:** Beginner **TIME:** 1–2 hours

MATERIALS NEEDED:

- Green paper
- Pink paper
- Flower punch
- 5 x 7 in. (12.5 x 17.5 cm) white blank card
- Eyelet tool and gold eyelets
- Assorted fibers

- Needle
- Acid-free adhesive
- 3½ x 4¼-in. (9 x 11-cm) photo
- Yellow card
- Craft knife, cutting mat, and ruler

1 Cut one pink and one green piece of paper 5 in. (12.5 cm) square. Punch three flowers equally spaced across the top of the piece of green paper with a craft punch.

2 Layer the papers with green uppermost, at the base of the card front. Using an eyelet tool, punch holes down both sides and at the bottom of the card. Fix an eyelet in each hole.

3 Thread assorted fibers through the eyelets, tying knots in the ends at both top corners and in the center bottom.

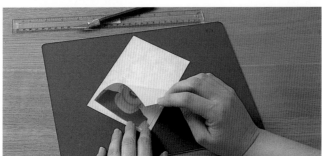

4 Mount the photo at the bottom of a 4 x 6-in. (10 x 15-cm) piece of yellow card with acid-free adhesive, leaving an equal border at the bottom and both sides.

5 Punch out three flowers from the remaining pink paper and glue them in position across the top of the yellow card.

6 Stamp or write a personalized message on the front of the pocket if you wish and insert the mounted photo inside.

CRAFTER'S TIP

If you make sure that you use acid-free papers and adhesive to make your card, the recipient can incorporate it in his or her own scrapbook. This is a great way to exchange photos between friends and family.

Christmas tea-bag card

Tea-bag folding has become very popular over the last few years, and there are many specially made papers for this craft. However, this simple but attractive card was made using lightweight decorative Christmas paper. You could even use a Christmas wrapping paper with a small design to great effect. And why not also make wreaths to decorate your Christmas tree?

TECHNIQUE: Tea-bag folding **LEVEL:** Beginner **TIME:** 1–2 hours

MATERIALS NEEDED:
- Lightweight Christmas paper
- PVA glue
- White 3 x 8-in. (7.5 x 20-cm) blank card
- Green script paper
- Double-sided tape
- Thin red ribbon
- Craft knife, cutting mat, ruler, and scissors

1 Cut eight 1½-in. (3-cm) squares of Christmas paper. Fold each square in half, patterned side out, and open out again. Fold the corners at one end into the center line.

2 Fold in half again, along the fold line created in Step 1. Fold the opposite corner up, as shown, to create a pocket. Make sure you fold all the squares in the same direction.

3 To make the Christmas wreath, put a touch of PVA glue on the point of each piece and insert it into the pocket of another. Join all eight pieces of paper in this way.

4 Close the white card blank. Cut a 3 x 6-in. (7.5 x 15-cm) piece of green script paper. Wrap it around the top of the white card, securing with double-sided tape. Trim the excess with a knife and rule. Repeat with a strip ⅜ in. (1 cm) wide near the base of the card.

5 Thread a loop of ribbon around the wreath and fix to the top of the card with PVA glue, as shown.

6 Tie a small red ribbon bow and glue in position to hide the ends of the ribbon fixing.

Accordion card

The art of harmonica folding is relatively simple, but the end result can be amazing. As with all greetings cards, the options are endless — here pretty decoupage pansies have been layered with ribbled (corrugated) and glitter card, perfect for a spring birthday or Mothers' Day.

TECHNIQUE: Paper folding, decoupage, and ribbling **LEVEL:** Intermediate **TIME:** 2–3 hours

MATERIALS NEEDED:

- Pale green and pale blue card
- Harmonica hexagon template
- Pansy decoupage paper
- Yellow glitter card
- Double-sided tape
- Sticky foam pads
- Scissors
- Ribbler
- Embossing tool
- Craft knife, cutting mat, and ruler

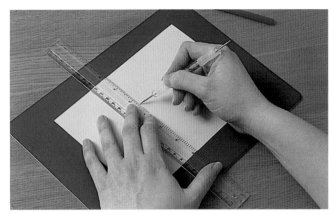

1 Cut an 8½ x 5⅞-in. (21 x 13-cm) piece of pale green card. Measure 3½ in. (9 cm) along the long edge and score the card.

2 Turn the card over (top to bottom). Measure 1¾ in. (4 cm) from the left edge and cut a single hexagon and score the fold. Measure 6 in. (15 cm) from the left edge and cut the two hexagons, scoring the fold.

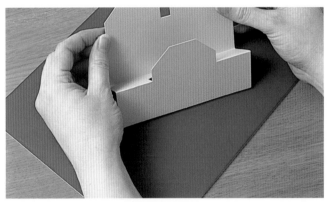

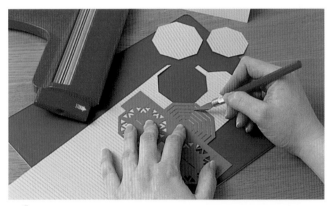

3 Fold the card along the score lines, being careful to avoid the hexagons.

4 Ribble a length of pale blue card and, using the template as a guide, cut three complete hexagons, one 2⅜ in. (3.5 cm) wide and two 1¹⁵⁄₁₆ in. (5 cm) wide.

5 Cut the assorted small pansies from the decoupage paper and layer the larger single pansy square using sticky foam pads. Cut one 1⅜-in. (3.5-cm) square and two 1³⁄₁₆-in. (3-cm) squares from yellow glitter card. Stick the large single pansy square and the two small pansy squares on the yellow glitter squares.

6 Layer the two small pansy squares on the two small ribbled hexagons in the back two card hexagons. Stick the larger single pansy on the large ribbled hexagon beneath the three little pansies in the front hexagon. Finish with two little pansies in the top corners of the front of the card.

Origami card

Origami is a very ancient form of paper folding and is used here to make a greeting card with a difference. The paper flowers are very small but look delightful when made in pearlescent paper. Just remember, "less is more" in Japanese flower arranging!

TECHNIQUE: Origami **LEVEL:** Intermediate **TIME:** 2–3 hours

MATERIALS NEEDED:

- Lightweight pearlescent yellow textured paper
- Circle aperture square cream card
- White paper
- Patterned vase die cut with glue pad
- Decorating chalks
- Cinnamon and khaki three-dimensional paint
- 0.3 mm ultrafine metal nib
- Double-sided tape
- Scissors
- Craft knife, cutting mat, and ruler

1 First make the flowers. Cut three 1⅜-in. (3.5-cm) squares of pearlescent yellow paper. Fold in half diagonally, corner to corner, both ways, opening out again each time.

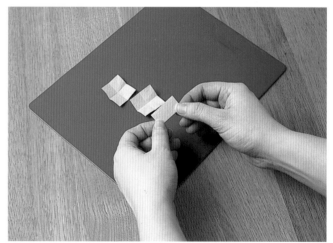

2 Then fold each square edge to edge (to make a rectangular shape), both ways, again opening out each time back to the original square shape.

3 Using the fold lines, push two opposite corners into the center to create a diamond shape.

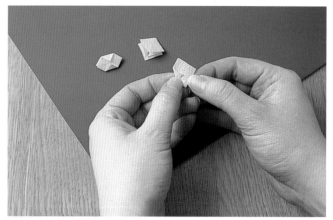

4 Fold the two outer points of the front of the diamond into the center. Flip it over and repeat on the back.

5 Fold the bottom points into the center, again repeating on the back.

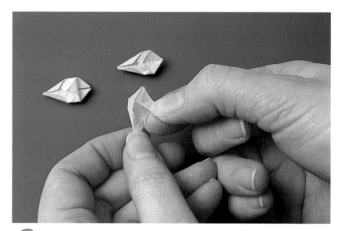

6 Carefully curl the front top flap out and down. Repeat Steps 1 to 5 with the remaining squares.

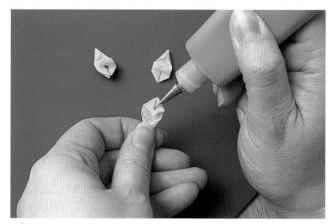

7 Using a fine nib, gently squeeze a small blob of cinnamon three-dimensional paint into the center of each folded flower to look like the stamens. Let the paint dry for an hour.

8 To make the card background, take a piece of white paper and apply some yellow, green, and purple decorating chalks, as shown, blending them with your finger.

9 Using double-sided tape, fix the background paper in the circle aperture card so the colored side shows at the front of the card. Stick the ready-glued vase die cut over the bottom edge.

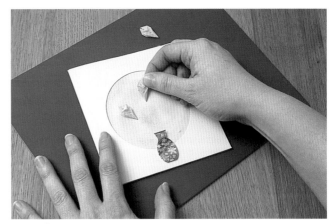

10 Use more small pieces of double-sided tape to fix the three flowers in position.

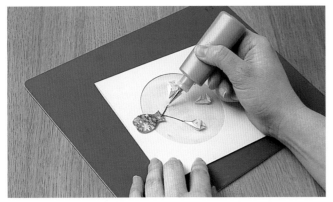

11 With khaki three-dimensional paint and a fine nib, draw stalks from the base of each flower into the top of the vase.

12 Using the same paint, draw some tall leaves coming up from the vase.

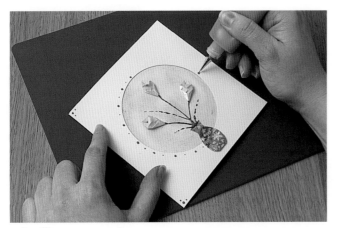

13 Create little dots at regular intervals around the circular aperture and in the corners with cinnamon three-dimensional paint; then let dry.

CRAFTER'S TIP

The more precise you are when cutting the origami squares and folding the papers, the better the finished flowers will look, so take your time and practice the folds.

Shaker card

Shaker aperture cards can be rather expensive to buy, so here are instructions for making your own. You can use any card to create a shaker card, whether it has an aperture or not. Here a blank card has been used and a pocket for the shaker pieces created using foam strips, double-sided tape, and acetate, with some gorgeous origami paper used for the background.

TECHNIQUE: Window making **LEVEL:** Intermediate **TIME:** 1–2 hours

MATERIALS NEEDED:

- 4-in. (10-cm) square of decorative paper
- 2 ⅜-in. (6-cm) square of pearlescent paper
- 5 in. (12.5 cm) blank pink square card
- Double-sided tape (standard and narrow)
- Frosted shrink plastic
- Horseshoe stamp
- Gold ink pad
- Pink pencil
- Eyelet punch tool
- Scissors
- Heat embossing tool or oven
- Pink card
- Decorative-edged scissors
- Acetate
- White foam
- Crystal glitter
- Small heart confetti
- Sequin flowers
- PVA glue
- Craft knife, cutting mat, and ruler

1 Using double-sided tape, layer the squares of decorative paper and pearlescent paper in the center of the blank pink card. Cut out three 3-in. (7.5-cm) squares of frosted shrink plastic.

2 Stamp the horseshoe pattern onto the matte side of the plastic with gold ink. Color in the ribbon with pink pencil. Punch small holes in the horseshoe with the eyelet tool and then cut out. Make two more.

3 Following the manufacturer's instructions, put the horseshoes in an oven or lay them on a heat-resistant surface and use a heat tool to shrink them. While still warm, flatten with the back of the stamp.

4 Use a craft knife and ruler to cut a 3-in. (7.5-cm) square of pink card with a 2-in. (5-cm) square aperture in the center. Trim the outside edges with decorative-edged scissors.

5 Stick narrow double-sided tape all around the aperture on the reverse of the card. Position a 2¾-in. (7-cm) square of acetate over the top.

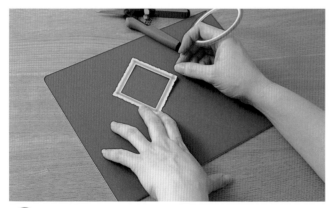

6 Stick more double-sided tape on each side of the aperture, making sure that you overlap the corners and position it approximately ¹⁄₁₆ in. (1 mm) in from the inner edge.

7 Using a craft knife and ruler, cut ⅕-in. (5-mm)-wide strips of white foam. Cut one strip to fit exactly across the bottom of the aperture to form a shelf.

8 Stick two more foam strips up against the aperture and down each side, making sure that they tightly abut the first strip.

9 Stick the last strip across the top, cutting it slightly long and using scissors to push the end in for a tight fit.

10 Stick narrow double-sided tape all around the aperture on top of the foam. Again, overlap the corners and position it $\frac{1}{16}$ in. (1 mm) from the inner edge.

11 Take the pink card and place the shrunk horseshoes, some crystal glitter, and small heart confetti in the center of the pearl paper. Stick the pink frame with acetate and foam over the top, making sure the foam shelf is at the bottom.

12 Use small dabs of PVA glue to attach a small flower sequin in each corner of the card.

CRAFTER'S TIP

To create successful shaker cards, it is vital to use foam strips with double-sided tape rather than the sticky-foam tape. This is because when the glue is applied during manufacture, it makes the edges of the foam tacky too, so the first time the card is shaken, all the pieces stick around the edges of the aperture, leaving nothing left to shake. By using foam strips, you can avoid this by placing the double-sided tape away from the edge of the foam.

Parchment wedding card

The marriage of a close friend or relative is a time for celebration. Show how much they mean to you by taking the time to make them this parchment wedding congratulations card. It will be one they will want to treasure as a memento of the day.

TECHNIQUE: Parchment craft **LEVEL:** Advanced **TIME:** 4–5 hours

MATERIALS NEEDED:

- Parchment vellum
- Magenta oil pastel
- Parchment blending oil or white spirit, tissue
- White ink
- Mapping pen
- Single-needle, four-needle, and heart-needle tools
- Small embossing tool
- Felt pad
- Parchment snips
- Curved parchment scissors
- 12 x 8¼-in. (30 x 21-cm) white pearlescent paper and card

- Pink gauze ribbon
- Vellum tape and small plastic vellum spatula
- Double-sided tape
- Sticky tape
- Low-tack masking tape
- Small piece of board or cutting mat
- Craft knife, cutting mat, and ruler

1 Photocopy the template on page 173 and lay a 6 x 8¼-in. (15 x 21-cm) piece of parchment vellum over the top. Lightly color the vellum along the edges of the template with the magenta oil pastel.

2 Put a drop of parchment oil or white spirit on a tissue and gently massage into the color, softening the edges. Wipe over the whole card, leaving a pale hue to the vellum center and a stronger pink border.

3 Turn the vellum over and fix it in position on the template with low-tack masking tape. Using the mapping pen and white ink, trace the teardrops around the border and the central design.

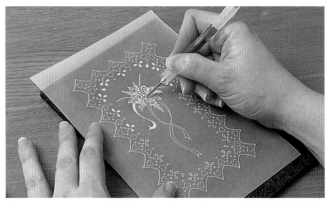

4 Place the vellum and attached template on the felt pad. Use the heart-needle tool to perforate the hearts, the four-needle tool to perforate the four-hole squares, and the single-needle tool to perforate all around the outer edge.

5 Remove the vellum from the template and turn it over facedown on the felt pad. Use the embossing tool to emboss the teardrops and the central design.

6 Lift the parchment from the felt pad and use the parchment snips to cut each side of the four-hole squares, creating small crosslike shapes.

7 Use the curved parchment scissors to cut around the outside of the design, making sure you cut through each perforation to give a decorative edge.

8 Take an 8¼ x 12-in. (21 x 30-cm) piece of pearlescent card, and use the embossing tool and ruler to score a fold line approximately 5⅛ in. (13 cm) along the long edge. Fold this in two and, using a craft knife, trim the card so that it measures 6⁷⁄₁₀ x 4³⁄₁₀ in. (17 x 11 cm). Cut an 8½ x 6½-in. (21.5 x 16.5-cm) piece of pearlescent paper and fold it in half.

9 Open up the card and position the vellum on the front. Carefully make two small incisions with a craft knife at each corner, along the inner edges of the hearts. Thread small pieces of ribbon through the vellum and card, and fix on the reverse side with tape. With double-sided tape, stick the pearlescent-paper insert on the back to cover the ribbon ends.

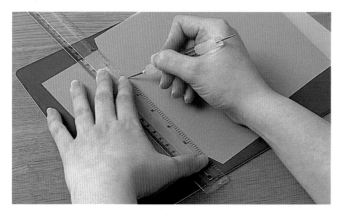

10 For the matching envelope, enlarge the template on page 173, and use to cut and score an 8½ x 12-in. (21 x 30-cm) piece of vellum.

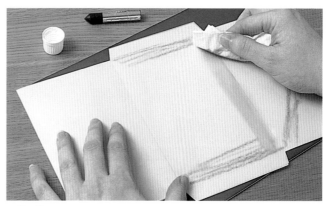

11 Apply magenta oil pastel on the inside of the envelope, around the edges of the front panel, across the edges of the flap, and across the base of the back panel. Use parchment oil to soften (as in Steps 1 to 2).

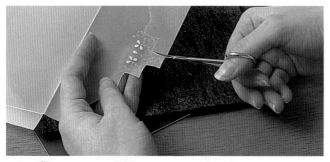

12 Position the flap over the design and follow Steps 3 to 7 to trace the teardrops, prick out the pattern, emboss the teardrops, snip the squares, and finish cutting the flap.

13 Apply vellum tape to the side flaps and rub lightly with a small spatula to transfer the glue onto the vellum. Peel off all the backing tape and fold up the back of the envelope.

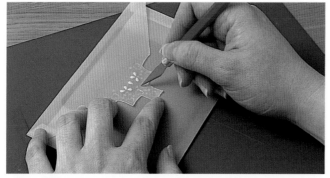

14 Place a piece of board or small cutting mat inside the envelope and fold the top flap down. With a craft knife, make two small cuts through the flap and back panel of the envelope along the edges of the two hearts. Remove the board and thread a length of ribbon through the slits in the back panel.

15 Cut a piece of pearlescent paper slightly smaller than 6⁹⁄₁₀ x 4½ in. (17.5 x 11.5 cm) and insert into the envelope. When you are ready to give your card, place it inside the envelope so that the front of the card is protected by the paper insert and close the envelope by tying it shut with the ribbon.

Templates

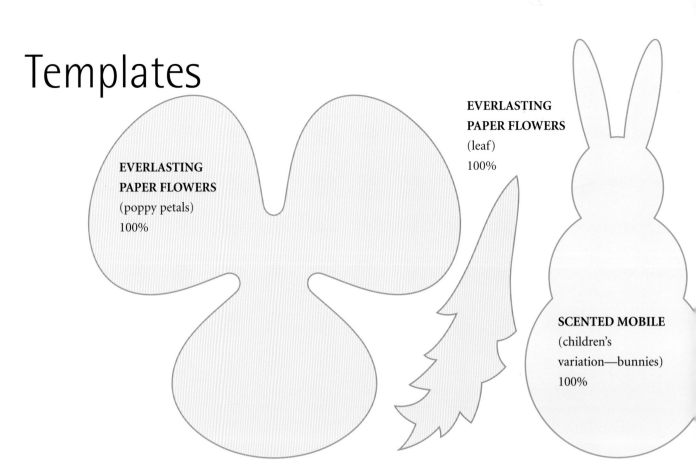

**EVERLASTING
PAPER FLOWERS**
(poppy petals)
100%

**EVERLASTING
PAPER FLOWERS**
(leaf)
100%

SCENTED MOBILE
(children's
variation—bunnies)
100%

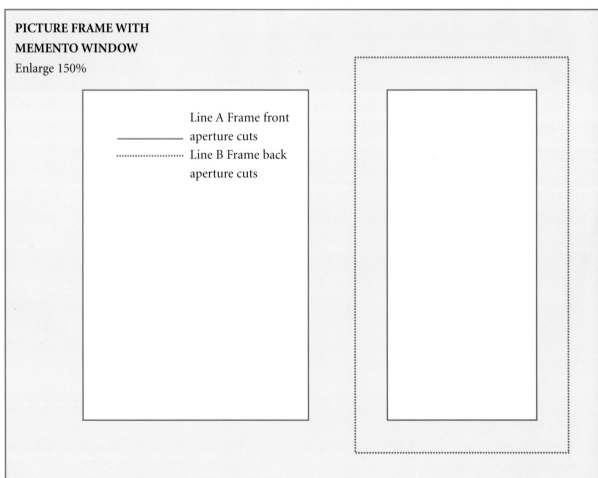

**PICTURE FRAME WITH
MEMENTO WINDOW**
Enlarge 150%

Line A Frame front
aperture cuts

Line B Frame back
aperture cuts

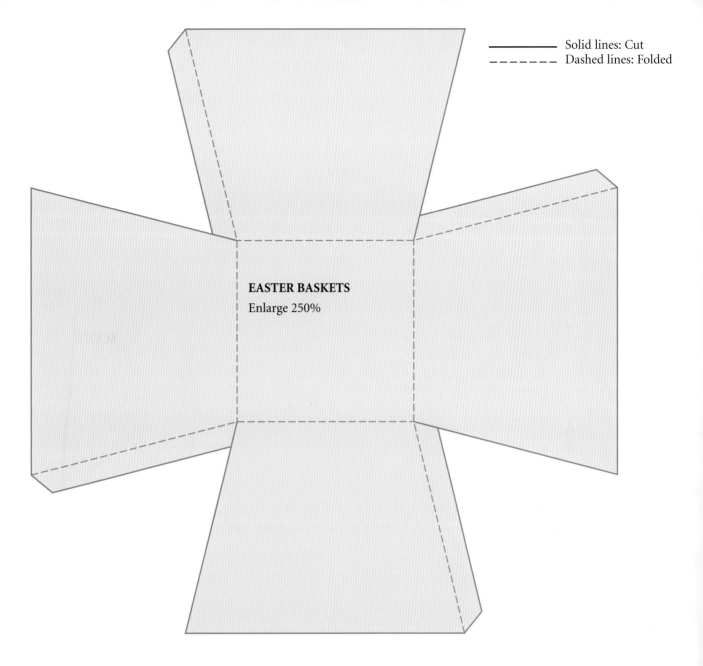

Solid lines: Cut
Dashed lines: Folded

EASTER BASKETS
Enlarge 250%

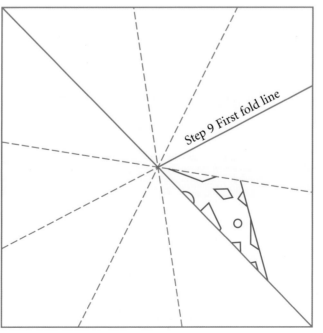

Step 9 First fold line

**3-D CHRISTMAS
DECORATIONS**
Enlarge 150%

Blue lines = cut marks when
folded

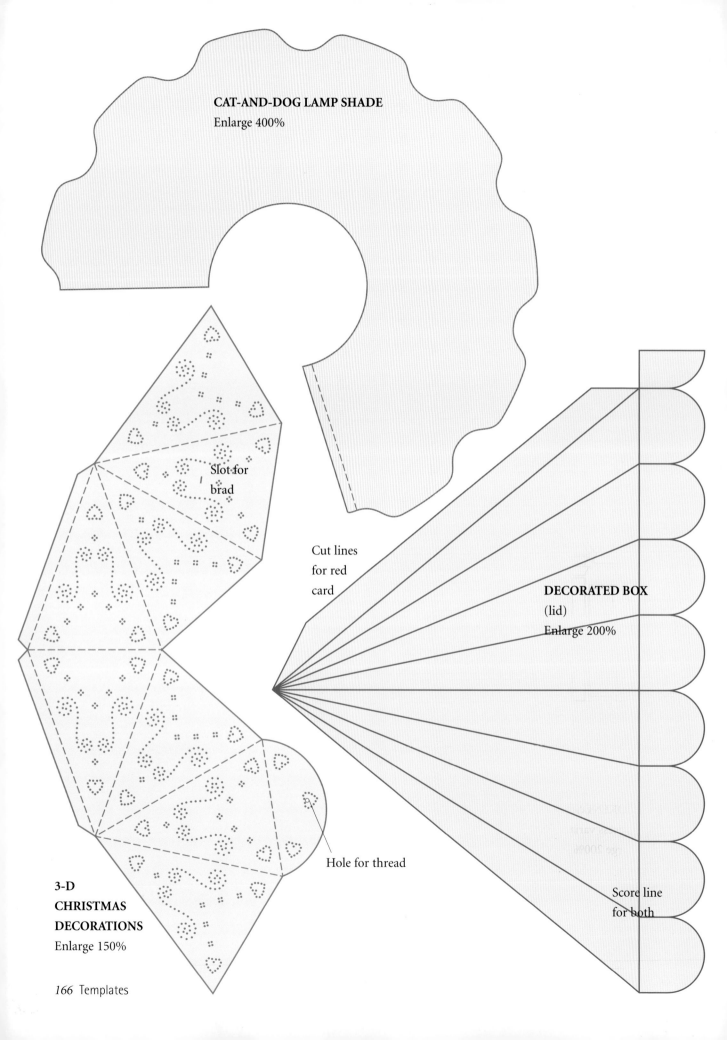

CAT-AND-DOG LAMP SHADE

Enlarge 400%

Slot for
brad

Cut lines
for red
card

DECORATED BOX
(lid)
Enlarge 200%

Hole for thread

**3-D
CHRISTMAS
DECORATIONS**

Enlarge 150%

Score line
for both

BOOKENDS

Enlarge 200%

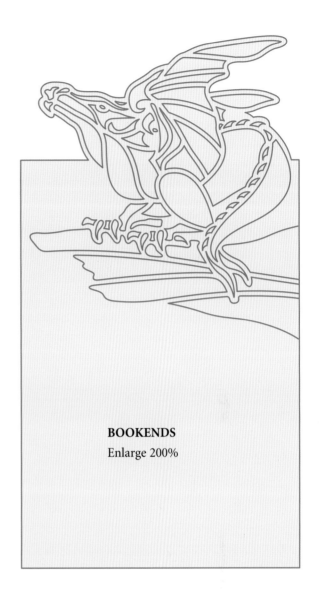

BOOKENDS

Enlarge 200%

BOOKENDS

(princess variation)

Enlarge 200%

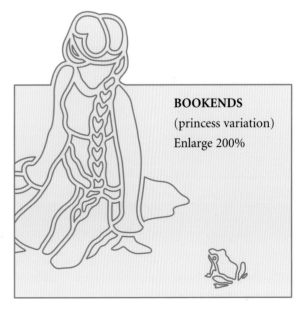

BOOKENDS

(princess variation)

Enlarge 200%

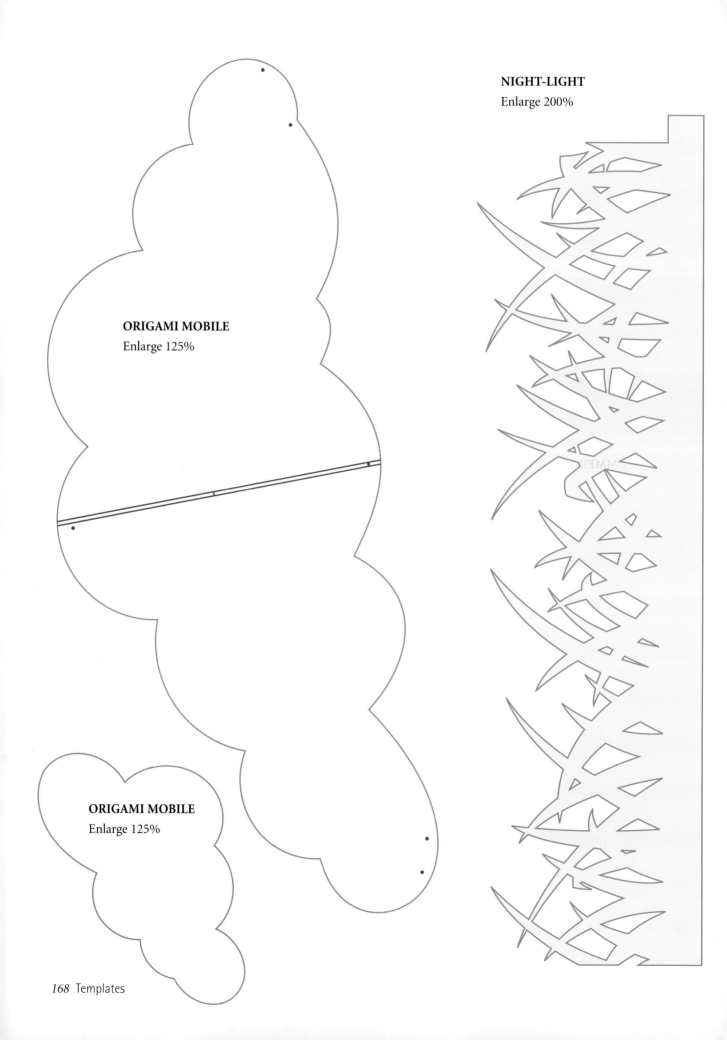

NIGHT-LIGHT
Enlarge 200%

ORIGAMI MOBILE
Enlarge 125%

ORIGAMI MOBILE
Enlarge 125%

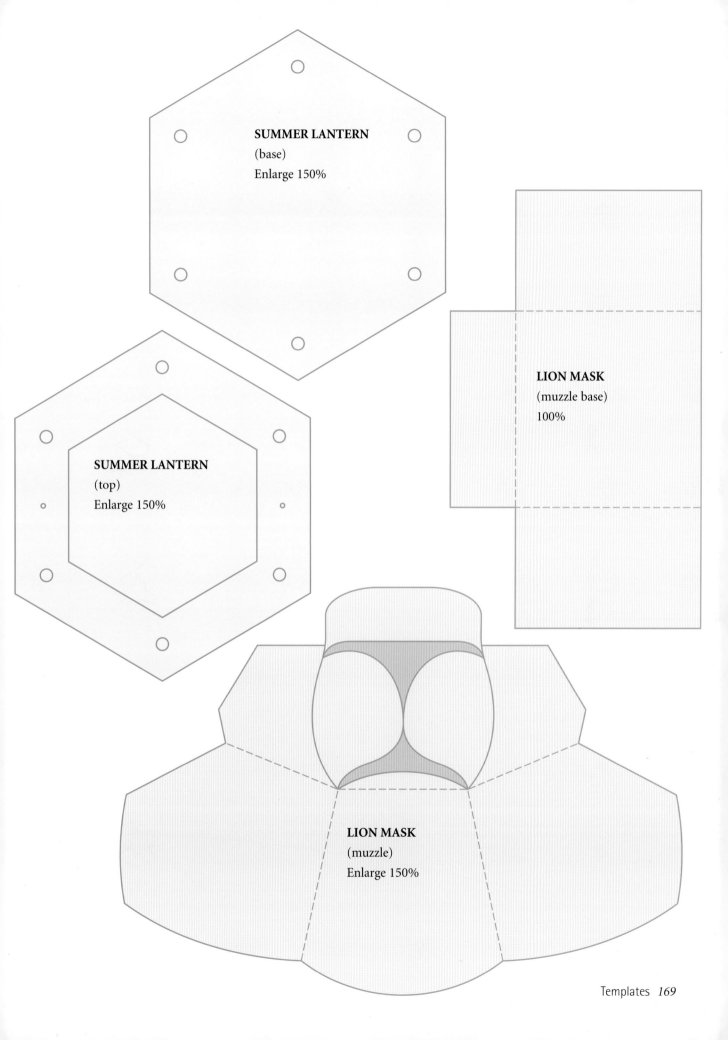

SUMMER LANTERN
(base)
Enlarge 150%

LION MASK
(muzzle base)
100%

SUMMER LANTERN
(top)
Enlarge 150%

LION MASK
(muzzle)
Enlarge 150%

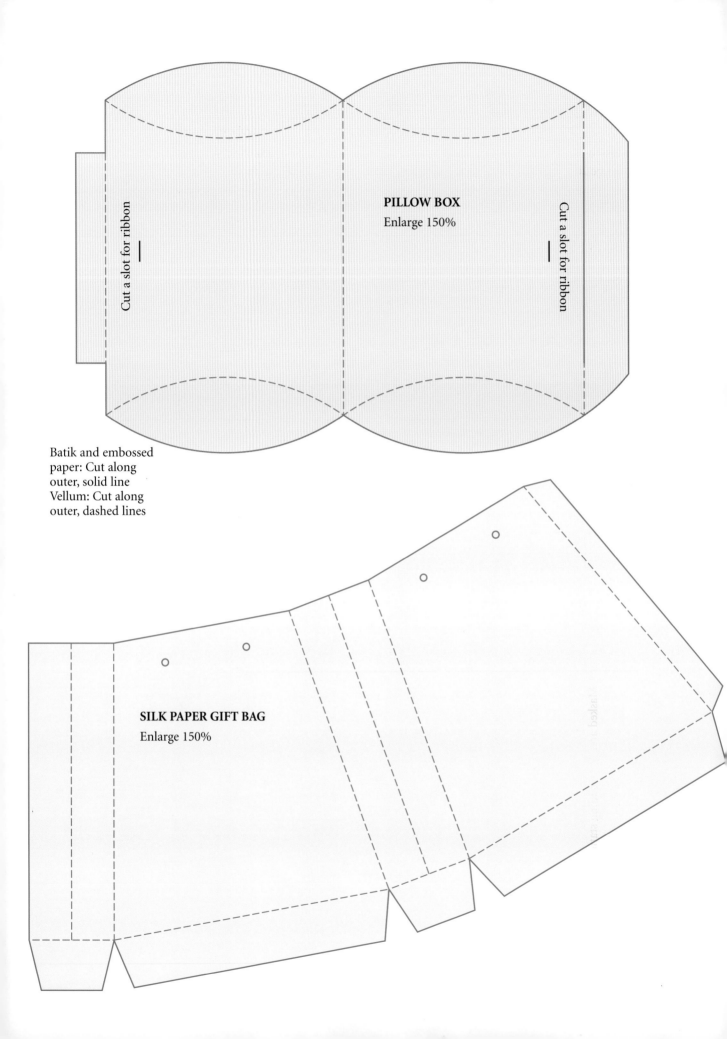

PILLOW BOX
Enlarge 150%

Cut a slot for ribbon

Cut a slot for ribbon

Batik and embossed
paper: Cut along
outer, solid line
Vellum: Cut along
outer, dashed lines

SILK PAPER GIFT BAG
Enlarge 150%

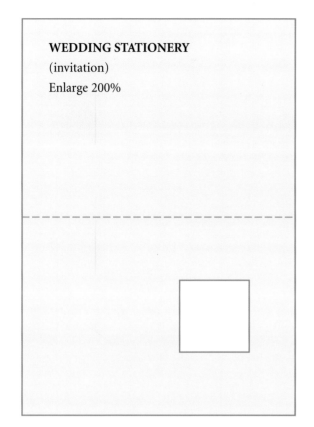

WEDDING STATIONERY
(invitation)
Enlarge 200%

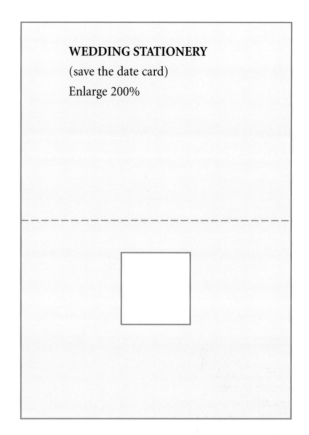

WEDDING STATIONERY
(save the date card)
Enlarge 200%

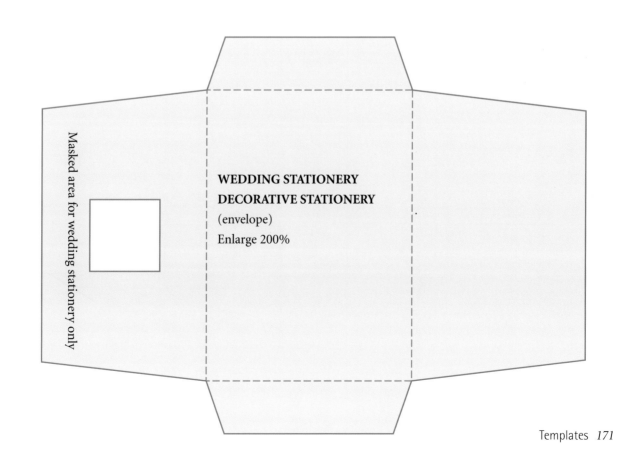

Masked area for wedding stationery only

WEDDING STATIONERY
DECORATIVE STATIONERY
(envelope)
Enlarge 200%

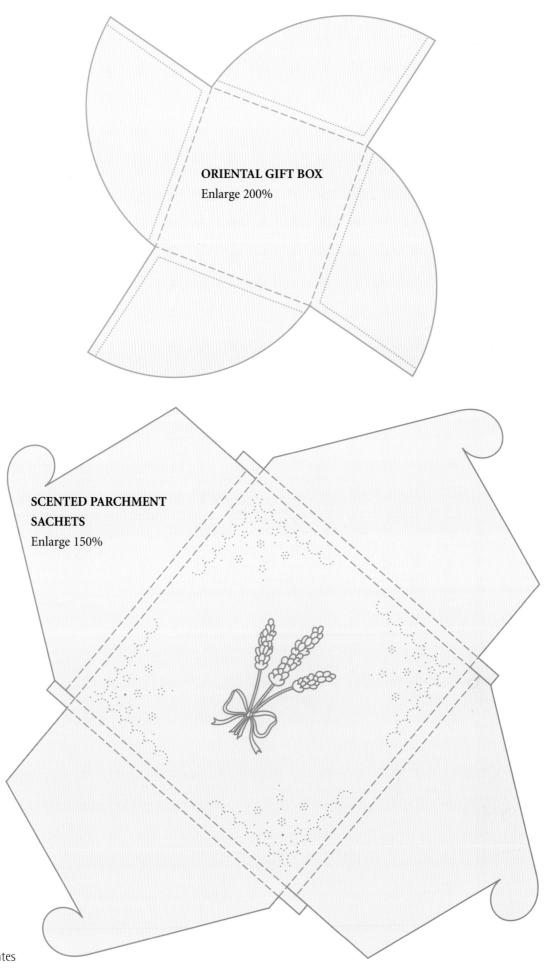

ORIENTAL GIFT BOX
Enlarge 200%

**SCENTED PARCHMENT
SACHETS**
Enlarge 150%

CELEBRATION CARD

100%

CELEBRATION CARD

Enlarge 400%

PARCHMENT WEDDING CARD

(envelope)

Enlarge 200%

PARCHMENT WEDDING CARD

100%

Glossary

Acid-free glue, paper, and card Used in scrapbooking to prevent pages from discoloring and disintegrating over time.

Altered art The technique of taking a mundane, everyday object and turning it into a work of art.

Brad A metal fastener used to hold several pieces of paper together. There are many decorative brads available for crafting projects, either as fasteners or purely for decoration.

Cotton linters Sheets of dried cotton pulp that can be reconstituted by soaking in water. A quick-and-easy pulp, ideal for papermaking and casting.

Countersink A carpenter's tool that gives a beveled edge to a predrilled hole.

Decorating chalks Available in a paint-palette format for ease of use for craft applications.

Decoupage The art of cutting out pictures and applying them to objects for decoration. 3-D decoupage is a variation where several copies of the same picture are layered, each subsequent layer consisting of smaller details of the original picture.

Die-cut machine A basic machine that requires a metal die to punch out the required shape from paper or lightweight card. The quickest, neatest, and easiest way of cutting out intricate shapes from paper.

Dry adhesive Available in stick form, it is applied by hand to the surface to be glued. Alternatively, it can be purchased as sheets or cassettes for different application machines that will apply a uniform layer of adhesive to the surface.

Dye ink pad Water-based ink pad designed for rubber stamping. When applied to paper, the ink dries very quickly. If it gets wet, the ink will reactivate and run. If applied to a glossy surface, it will take longer to dry, allowing time for embossing.

Embossing tool A wooden- or plastic-handled tool with different-sized metal balls at either end. Designed for embossing and scoring paper, card, and sheet metal.

Essential oil An aromatherapy oil that can be used to scent paper when papermaking, or in other craft applications, such as candle making and soap making.

Eyelet A small, typically metal ring used to reinforce a hole. A wide variety of shapes, colors, and sizes are available as craft embellishments.

Gilding wax A metalic wax mainly used to embellish wooden picture frames. It can be applied to many surfaces, even card, provided it is used sparingly.

Harmonica template A metal template or stencil that is designed to allow crafters to cut accordion or harmonica cards. Available in a variety of geometric shapes.

Heat-embossing tool A tool used to melt embossing powder that has been applied to a stamped image. It has other craft applications, such as shrinking plastic, melting ultra-thick embossing powders, and puffing up some three-dimensional paints.

Kirigami The art of paper folding and cutting to create intricate designs.

Lickable glue A glue that can be applied to paper and, when dry, can be reactivated by moistening. A perfect glue for the flaps of handmade paper envelopes.

Low-tack tape A lightly glued tape that can be purchased in repositionable or standard form. It is ideal for use with more delicate papers.

Marbling A method of transferring an inked pattern to paper. Oil- and water-based marbling inks are available. Inks are dropped onto the carrier solution, a pattern is then created before laying a piece of paper over the top to transfer the design.

Masking tape A low-tack paper tape that can be easily torn and used to section off areas or temporarily fix items in position.

Matting A scrapbooking term where different-sized papers are layered, usually as a backing for a photograph.

Metal leaf Real or imitation metal leaf is available. Imitation leaf is cheaper but must be varnished to stop it from tarnishing with time.

Mica Colored or transparent mineral silicates that readily separate into very thin leaves. They can be bought as flakes or as larger pieces.

Mountboard A thick card available in many colors, initially used for mounting pictures.

Mulberry paper This fibrous paper is slightly thicker than tissue paper but can still be easily pulled apart when water is applied to it, giving it a delicate, feathery edge.

Origami The ancient Japanese art of paper folding, which has been in existence for hundreds of years.

Paper casting A technique of creating decorative embossed paper using either a clay casting mold or alternative mold, such as a rubber stamp.

Papier-mâché A method of creating a strong, lightweight paper shape by covering a mold with scrap paper and glue.

Pigment ink pad Glycerine-based ink pads designed for rubber stamping and embossing. The ink takes some time to dry because it can only soak into the surface, thereby allowing the stamper to emboss it if desired. If applied to a glossy surface, it must be embossed because it will never dry completely.

PVA glue An adhesive that contains a colorless resin. It must be able to soak into both surfaces to create a bond. Purchase a crafter's PVA rather than a school or children's PVA, which has a higher water content.

Quilling The craft of curling thin strips of colored paper into shapes and arranging them to make a pattern or picture. Three-dimensional shapes can also be created.

Ribbler A small handheld machine that consists of two shaped metal rollers through which card and paper are passed to create a corrugated effect. Embossing ribblers are available that create embossed patterns.

Shrink plastic A sheet of plastic that can be rubber stamped and drawn on. Once cut out, it can be placed in an ordinary domestic oven or heated with a rubber-stamping heat-embossing tool to shrink 7 times smaller, 7 times thicker.

Silicone glue A glue with water-resistant qualities used mainly for 3-D decoupage.

Spray webbing A special paint in a spray can that has a stringlike quality. When sprayed across a page, it can give dramatic weblike effects. Available in a limited number of colors.

Stencil cutting tool A fine metal-tipped, electrically heated tool used to cut intricate designs in acetate. Place the design under a piece of glass and lay the acetate on top before tracing the design with the heated tool.

Tea-bag folding The art of folding small squares of paper and then assembling them into intricate patterns for a decorative effect.

Three-dimensional paint A paint that retains its shape when applied to a surface.

Vellum One of the oldest papers, now commercially manufactured by machine. It has translucent qualities and is available in a variety of colors and patterns. There are specialized inks designed for use with vellum that are applied with a brush or pen.

Washi paper Made in Japan, it can be delicately patterned with fibers and is a very tough paper despite being lightweight.

Resources

My thanks go to John Wright of Pébèo UK Ltd, William Weil of Sinotex UK Ltd, and Martin Erler of Efco for their support. Thanks also to Marij Rahder, Christine Haworth, Jalekro, Anna Griffin, Inkadinkado, Stamp Oasis, Express Services, Craft Creations, and Design Objectives for their kind permission to allow me to use their stamps and decoupage papers in this book. My sincere thanks go to everyone else who helped and advised me along the way.

The following products were used in the projects:

Advent Calender Base by Efco
www.efco.de

Blank Scrapbook by K and Company
distributed in the UK by Personal Impressions
www.kandcompany.com
www.richstamp.co.uk

Cat, Dog, and Paw Stamps and Small Flower Stamps by Design Objectives
www.docrafts.co.uk

Clown Decoupage Print by Craft Creations
www.craftcreations.co.uk

Coaster by Framecraft Miniatures
www.framecraftminatures.co.uk

Fan Stamp by Stamp Oasis
www.stampoasis.com

Faerie Poppet Decoupage Paper by Christine Haworth
manufactured by Jalekro, distributed by Kars
www.jalekro.co
www.kars.nl

Flower Basket Stamp and Initial Stamp by Anna Griffin
www.annagriffin.com

Microwavable Silk Dyes by Arty's
www.artys.co.uk

Old Car Stamp by Hobby Art Stamps
www.sirstampalot.co.uk

Pansy Decoupage Paper by Marij Rahder
distributed in Europe by Kars
www.kars.nl

Papermaking Frame by Kundalini
distributed by West Design Products Limited
www.westdesign.co.uk

Snowflake Stamp by Inkadinkado
distributed in the UK by Bramwell Yarns and Crafts
www.bramwell.co.uk

MANUFACTURERS/DISTRIBUTORS—USA
Fiskars Brands, Inc.
www.fiskars.com

Hot off the Press
www.craftpizazz.com

K and Company
www.kandcampany.com

Making Memories
www.makingmemories.com

Paper Adventures
www.paperadventures.com

QuicKutz, Inc.
www.quickutz.com

Sissix
www.sissix.com

Stamp Oasis
www.stampoasis.com

Tsukineko, Inc.
www.tsukineko.com

MANUFACTURERS/DISTRIBUTORS—Europe
Craft Creations
www.craftcreations.co.uk

Efco
www.efco.de

Design Objectives
www.docrafts.co.uk

Express Services
www.expressrubberstamps.co.uk

F W Bramwell and Co Ltd
www.bramwellcrafts.co.uk

Framecraft Miniatures
www.framecraftminatures.co.uk

The Handmade Paper Company
www.handmadepaper.co.uk

IHR Ideal Home Range
www.idealhomerange.com

Kars.UK
www.kars.nl

The Paper Shed
www.papershed.com

Paperstate
www.paperstate.co.uk

Pébèo UK Ltd
www.pebeo.com

Personal Impressions
www.richstamp.co.uk

Royal Brush Manufacturing (UK) Ltd
www.royalbrush.com

Sinotex UK Ltd
www.artys.co.uk

G F Smith
www.gfsmith.com

West Design Products Limited
www.westdesign.co.uk

RETAILERS—USA
Beadworks
www.beadworks.com

Arnold Grummer
www.arnoldgrummer.com

Herrschners, Inc.
www.herrschners.com

Michaels Stores, Inc.
Tel:1-800-MICHAELS (1-800-642-4235)

Quilled Creations
www.quilledcreations.com

RETAILERS—Europe
Advanced Crafts
www.advancedcrafts.co.uk

Art Van Go
www.artvango.co.uk

The Bead Shop
www.beadshop.co.uk

Card Inspirations
www.cardinspirations.co.uk

Chameleon Crafts
www.chameleoncrafts.co.uk

Craft Art UK
www.craftartuk.com

Creative World
www.creativeworld.co.uk

Gadsby's
www.artshopper.co.uk

Francis Iles
www.artycat.com

The Mulberry Bush
www.themulberry-bush.com

The Papertrail Scrapbook Company
www.goscrapbook.co.uk

Purple Planet
www.purpleplanet.co.uk

The Scrapbookhouse
www.thescrapbookhouse.com

Shillbrook Creative Crafts
www.shillbrook.co.uk

Sir Stampalot
www.sirstampalot.co.uk

Stampasaurus
www.stampasaurus.co.uk

Index